PUTIN'S RESET

The Bear is Back and How America Must Respond

Fred Fleitz, Editor
Stephen Blank
Kevin Freeman
Frank J. Gaffney, Jr.
Daniel Gouré
Cliff Kincaid
Roger W. Robinson, Jr.
David Satter
Mark B. Schneider
J. Michael Waller

Center for Security Policy Press

ISBN-13: 978-1539873143
ISBN-10: 1539873145

Putin's Reset: The Bear is Back and How America Must Respond
is published in the United States by the Center for Security Policy Press,
a division of the Center for Security Policy

November 4, 2016

THE CENTER FOR SECURITY POLICY
1901 Pennsylvania Avenue, NW, Suite 201, Washington, DC 20006
Phone: (202) 835-9077 | Email: info@securefreedom.org
For more information, please see securefreedom.org

Book Design by Adam Savit
Cover Design by J.P. Zarruk

Table of Contents

Foreword

By Frank J. Gaffney, Jr.

At no time since the fall of the Soviet Union has the threat from Russia been as serious – and Washington's relations with Moscow been as poor – as in the fall of 2016. As charges fly that Russia is trying to influence the outcome of the 2016 presidential election by leaking Democratic e-mails and Hillary Clinton and Donald Trump accuse each other of having inappropriate ties to the Russian government, the questions about where Vladimir Putin is taking his country and what that will mean for ours have largely gone unasked, let alone answered. *Putin's Reset: The Bear is Back and How America Must Respond* is an effort to address just such questions, drawing upon the expertise of some of the most competent and creative Russian hands and security policy practitioners of our time.

Thanks in part to the malfeasance of the Obama administration – evident in its initial, doomed effort to "reset" relations with the Kremlin and what flowed from it – Russia has become a major player in the Middle East over the last eight years and is expanding its influence at the expense of the United States. Moscow is forging new alliances around the world to promote its influence and undermine the United States, especially with China and Iran. Russia's growing influence and the perception that it is a more reliable power than the United States has even led Israeli Prime Minister Netanyahu to strengthen Israel's ties to Russia.

At the same time, there have been major improvements in Russia's ballistic missiles, air defenses and strategic and tactical nuclear forces. Moscow is improving its navy and striking deals for port access for its fleet around the world. Russia has deployed one of its most advanced missile systems in Syria to help protect and secure victory for its partner, the genocidal Bashar al-Assad. It also has sold advanced ground-to-air missiles to Iran, which Tehran is using to prevent possible Israeli and even U.S. airstrikes against a facility likely continuing the mullahs' clandestine nuclear bomb-making program.

The days of Russia's almost comical invasion of Georgia in 2008 – when Russian troops crossed the border sitting on top of dilapidated armored personnel carriers – are over. Today, the Red Army was on display with its stealthy and swift seizure in 2014 of Crimea by special operations forces and, subsequently, similar initiatives aimed at intervening in and subverting the pro-Western government of Ukraine.

Russia is increasingly using its military to threaten and menace the United States and U.S. allies, as well. Russian jets have been harassing American naval vessels and planes. Russian jets and bombers have infringed on the air space of the United States, Canada, Turkey, Estonia, Latvia, Lithuania, Finland and Sweden, among others. These incidents are raising fears by some former Soviet states that the Russian military could soon meddle in their countries as it has in Ukraine.

It is hard to overstate the cumulative impact and portentousness of all these actions. In his contribution to this collection of essays, noted Russia expert Dr. Stephen Blank depicts the situation with this grim warning: "Putin's Russia is preparing for war against the U.S. and NATO. Putin would prefer to win without fighting, but he is prepared to use force and apparently escalate to nuclear weapons use if it is necessary and in Russia's interests. He must be deterred. We are not doing nearly enough to do so."

The other distinguished national security experts who contributed to this book have reached a similar conclusion: the threat from Russia is growing as it gears up, at best, for a do-over of the Cold War. At worst, it is creating what the Soviets used to call "a correlation of forces" that will enable the Kremlin to engage decisively in actual hostilities against the United States.

- The editor of this collection, career intelligence professional and Center for Security Policy Senior Vice President Fred Fleitz, documents how Russia's strategic influence and relative power has been greatly magnified over the past eight years. He shows how these ominous trends have been fueled, in part, by the weakness and irresolution President Obama manifested towards Putin during his first term – and the fulfillment of the promise he made to the Russian dictator to be "more flexible" after his reelection.
- Former senior Pentagon official Dr. Mark B. Schneider analyzes in detail Russia's major strides in modernizing and expanding its nuclear arms and their array of delivery systems – including especially worrying ones involving more advanced thermonuclear weapon designs, hypersonic and maneuvering warheads and drone submarines.
- This trajectory is made the more alarming as it has been accompanied, on the one hand, by repeated threats to use such weapons emanating from Putin and, on the other, by the wholesale atrophying of America's

strategic and tactical nuclear arsenals. The confidence we, our allies and prospective enemies have in the U.S. deterrent is being further eroded by the dramatic improvements Russia has made in its air and missile defenses and in hardening and otherwise upgrading its underground bunker infrastructure, apparently in preparation for waging nuclear war.

- Another former senior Pentagon executive, Dr. Daniel Gouré, discusses Russian President Putin's strategy to use a revamped and modernized Russian military to achieve his goals of expanding his country's global influence at the expense of the United States, despite its serious financial and manpower limitations.

- Chartered Financial Analyst Kevin Freeman explains how Putin's Russia has very sophisticated economic weapons at its disposal, ranging from nation-ending options such as electro-magnetic pulse and cyber warfare to market manipulation, the coercive use of energy supplies and attacks on the U.S. dollar as the world's reserve currency. Freeman also examines the strategic implications of Russia's intensifying collaboration with China aimed at, among other goals, subverting America's global economic dominance.

- David Satter, a best-selling author, filmmaker, former journalist and acclaimed historian specializing in the Soviet Union and post-Soviet Russia, contributes chilling insights into the Vladimir Putin's character and ambitions, informed by his ruthless use of terror to acquire and hold power.

- Center for Security Policy Senior Fellow Dr. J. Michael Waller discusses Russia's formidable and growing information warfare operations. He addresses the cumulative effect of the Kremlin's propaganda infrastructure – including Putin's burgeoning use of the Internet, social media and Russia Today (RT), a Russian-government controlled cable news network, to disseminate seductive anti-American programing to audiences around the world. And,

- Former Reagan National Security Council official and economic and financial warfare expert Roger W. Robinson describes a potential flashpoint arising from Russia's seizure of Crimea and its imminent exploitation of what had been Ukraine's vast offshore oil and gas deposits in the Black Sea – and potentially those of Romania, as well.

- President of America's Survival and journalist Cliff Kincaid discusses whether the Soviet Union actually ended, the history of Soviet intelligence operations against the United States and Russia is continuing these operations today.

Our hope is that the American people, once equipped with such insights, will have a more complete understanding of how the Kremlin of yesteryear – with its global ambitions, bullying behavior and rabid hostility towards the United States immortalized by Candidate Ronald Reagan in a 1980 presidential campaign ad as "a bear in the woods" – is back. And, with that urgently needed understanding, the public will be better equipped to decide on what course is the most appropriate U.S. response: continued accommodation and appeasement or a return to the policy approach that Mr. Reagan as president employed to help bring down the Soviet Union: peace through strength.

Putin's Reset is a call to action, born of a shared conviction by its contributors that the Russian threat is very real. We have no more time for denial and political games by our elected officials. America has lost a lot of ground in terms of power and prestige to Vladimir Putin and other adversaries, most of whom are allied with him. Unless we take determined action to regain this ground starting now, America's vital interests and quite possibly the security of the American people could be at grave risk.

Frank J. Gaffney, Jr.
President and CEO
Center for Security Policy
24 October 2016

How Putin's Aggression Has Been Boosted by Obama's Weakness

By Fred Fleitz

"In short, we have every reason to assume that the infamous policy of containment, led in the 18th, 19th and 20th centuries, continues today. They are constantly trying to sweep us into a corner because we have an independent position, because we maintain it and because we call things like they are and do not engage in hypocrisy. But there is a limit to everything. And with Ukraine, our western partners have crossed the line, playing the bear and acting irresponsibly and unprofessionally."

-Russian President Vladimir Putin in a speech to a joint session of the Russian Parliament, March 18, 2014

Over the last few years, there have been several extraordinary instances of Russian disrespect and disregard for the United States and the U.S. president.

In March 2016, President Barack Obama hosted a summit of world leaders in Washington, DC to discuss one of Mr. Obama's foreign policy priorities: nuclear security and keeping nuclear weapons out of the hands of terrorists. Ordinarily, world leaders always attend such high-level events out of respect for the United States, especially when focused on a U.S. president's signature issue. However, Russia skipped the summit. A Russian official dismissed the meeting by saying, "We don't really know what the point of this summit is." This was a major snub of President Obama by President Putin.

In early September 2016, U.S. Secretary of State John Kerry and Russian Foreign Minister Sergey Lavrov negotiated a Syrian peace agreement that was supposed to result in a partial cease-fire. The agreement broke down after only two weeks after Russia, the Syrian government, and Iran ignored the agreement and intensified their attacks on Syrian rebels, especially in the besieged city of Aleppo. The U.S. response? Kerry condemned Russia for violating the peace agreement and said the United States would cease Syria talks with Russia.

There have been several reports of Russian jets flying dangerously close to U.S. planes and naval vessels over the last year. Last April in the Baltic Sea, U.S. ships experienced 31 fly-overs in a two day period. Although the Russian jets were not believed to be armed, the commander of one of the U.S. Navy ships subjected to the 31 fly-overs said the Russian jets used a "simulated attack profile."

These acts of Russian disrespect for the United States coincide with a sharp increase in Russian influence and belligerence since 2009 resulting from Russian President Vladimir Putin exploiting American weakness to reclaim for Russia much of the power and influence Moscow lost with the breakup of the Soviet Union. Later in this book, Dr. Stephen Blank explains what he views as the extreme seriousness of this development: "Putin's Russia is preparing for war against the U.S. and NATO."

A SOVIET AT HEART

It has long been known that Putin deeply regrets the fall of the Soviet Union. He has called the demise of the Soviet empire "the greatest geopolitical catastrophe of the century." Putin also has referred to the breakup as a "genuine tragedy" for Russians since tens of millions of his fellow countrymen suddenly found themselves living outside of Russia in new countries formed out of former Soviet republics.

Putin will state publically that he does not want to bring back the Soviet Union. In a 2015 Russian television documentary, he stated, "Russia is not trying to bring back the USSR, but nobody wants to believe it."[1]

Yet Putin frequently appeals to Russian nationalism by pledging to restore much of the greatness of the Soviet Union. Putin is pressing to create and gain international recognition of Russian spheres of influence among the former Soviet republic countries. According to Russian scholar Fiona Hill, "Putin has laid out his view that all the states that emerged from the USSR are appendages of Russia. They should pay fealty to Moscow."[2]

Coinciding with Putin's pining for the days of the Soviet Union is his preference for autocratic rule, distain for democracy and human rights, and an aggressive global campaign to undermine and counter American influence. These objectives stem not just from Putin being as essentially an unreformed Soviet-style autocrat at heart but also from his career as a KGB officer. Despite the ruthlessness and brutality of the Soviet intelligence services during the Cold War, Putin has been a staunch defender of Soviet-era intelligence agencies and essentially reincarnated the KGB in 2016.

Senator John McCain put it best when he said in a 2014 *New York Times* op-ed that Putin is "an unreconstructed Russian imperialist and KGB apparatchik."[3]

WAS RUSSIA BEHIND THE WIKILEAKS CONTROVERSY DURING THE 2016 PRESIDENTIAL ELECTION?

Throughout the 2016 presidential campaign there have been allegations that leaks of emails belonging to Democratic National Committee and Clinton campaign officials through WikiLeaks were stolen by Russian government hackers. Obama officials and the Clinton campaign constantly condemned these leaks as Russian interference in the 2016 election even though they never provided any clear evidence of Russian involvement.

On October 7, 2016, the Obama administration formally blamed Russia for these hacks, citing what it claimed was a determination by U.S. intelligence agencies that Moscow was behind them. To defend herself against the WikiLeaks disclosures, Hillary Clinton, in the third presidential debate on October 19, 2016, referred to this determination when she said:

> We have 17 intelligence agencies, civilian and military, who have all concluded that these espionage attacks, these cyberattacks, come from the highest levels of the Kremlin, and they are designed to influence our election.

What Obama officials and Clinton said about the public position of U.S. intelligence agencies on this issue was misleading. First of all, only two intelligence entities – the Office of the Director of National Intelligence (DNI) and the Department of Homeland Security (DHS) – weighed in on this issue, not 17 intelligence agencies. (There also are only 16 U.S. intelligence agencies, not 17.)

Second, the DNI/DHS memo on this issue was ambiguous about Russian involvement. The actual DNI/DHS statement said the hacks

> ... are consistent with the methods and motivations of Russian-directed efforts. These thefts and disclosures are intended to interfere with the US election process. Such activity is not new to Moscow — the Russians have used similar tactics and techniques across Europe and Eurasia, for example, to influence public opinion there. We believe, based on the scope and sensitivity of these

efforts, that only Russia's senior-most officials could have authorized these activities. [4]

U.S. intelligence officials saying that hacks of Democratic staff computers "are consistent with the methods and motivations of Russian-directed efforts" is far short of saying they have evidence that Russia is responsible for the hacks. High level officials might have authorized them if Russian hackers were responsible, but the DNI and DHS statement did not say there was evidence Russia was responsible.

Many experts doubt that US intelligence agencies know whether Russia was behind the hacks and believe there are other explanations for how they came about. However, the possibility of Russian involvement can't be ruled out. If Russia was involved, it would indicate a significant escalation in Putin's efforts to undermine the reputation of the United States and the U.S. political system.

HOW U.S. WEAKNESS HAS EMBOLDENED PUTIN

Putin's hostility towards a U.S.-dominated unipolar world and his desire to recapture at least some of the Soviet Union's greatness and influence for Russia has been known since the 1990s. The question in 2016 is why have Putin's efforts to expand Russian power and influence been so successful over the last eight years? The answer is simple: Putin has successfully taken advantage of one of the weakest American presidents in history – one who implemented policies of retreat and appeasement that created power vacuums and other opportunities that the Russian leader was easily able to exploit.

Putin also capitalized on the George W. Bush administration's weak policies during its second term when negative public sentiment over the Iraq war caused it to abandon the assertive policies of the first Bush term. This undermined America's credibility on the world stage and created a perception of weakness that was also exploited by other adversarial nations. For example, Iran began uranium enrichment during this period in violation of UN Security Council resolutions and North Korea conducted its first nuclear test in 2006, likely for similar reasons.

Global perception of American weakness has grown progressively worse during the Obama administration.

This started in 2009 with Obama foreign policy initiatives designed to move the United States away from the supposed overly belligerent "cowboy diplomacy" of the Bush years and instead adopt an approach based on consultations and multilateralism. This led to U.S. efforts to seek new diplomatic solutions with North

Korea and Iran and a slew apologies by President Obama to nearly every global audience – initially ranging from Europeans to the Muslim world and later to the citizens of Hanoi and Hiroshima – for what he considered "arrogant" previous U.S. policies.

Mr. Obama hoped this new approach would improve U.S. relations with its enemies and reduce the threat to the United States from Islamist terrorist groups. He was wrong. There was a huge increase in Iran's nuclear program between 2009 and 2013. Iran also tested long-range missiles believed to be prototype ICBMs. North Korea conducted its second nuclear test in May 2009 and expanded its missiles tests. The threat from Islamist terrorism grew. ISIS was born due to a resurgence in sectarian violence in Iraq that might have been avoided if President Obama had left a small contingent of U.S. troops behind when U.S. forces withdrew from Iraq at the end of 2011. The president's inept policies in Syria and Iraq – including a $500 million train-and-equip program to arm "moderate" Syrian rebels that he was forced to cancel -- worsened the crises in both states.

The Obama administration also began an effort to reset U.S.-Russia relations after what it claimed were overly confrontational policies of the Bush administration toward Russia. To announce this reset, Secretary of State Hillary Clinton presented Russian Foreign Minister Sergei Lavrov on March 6, 2009 with a box containing a symbolic "reset" button. Lavrov mocked Clinton when receiving the box because lettering, which she thought was the Russian word for reset actually was the Russian word "peregruzka" which means "overcharged."

Lavrov's mocking of Clinton over the translation mistake was probably the first public sign of the Putin government's disrespect for the Obama administration. It was followed by unyielding positions during talks to negotiate a follow-on agreement to the START I Treaty which expired in December 2009. The Obama administration's desperation for this agreement led it to abandon the "Third Site" missile defense initiative by scrapping plans to build missile defense facilities in Poland and the Czech Republic due to Russian opposition. This move alienated the Czech and Polish governments – both of which had resisted strong political pressure at home and from Moscow regarding their agreement to host the Third Site interceptors on their territories. More importantly, the Third Site cancellation was seen as America betraying its allies to appease Moscow. This weakness is, as Mark Schneider explains in this book, how Russia succeeded in making New START into the "treaty full of loopholes" it was looking for. This would lead to other U.S. humiliations as well.

HOW THE RUSSIAN RESET FAILED

Clinton's reset button gaffe took on more significance in the final years of the Obama administration as it became increasingly clear that Russian behavior on the international scene had significantly worsened and U.S.-Russia relations sank to the lowest level since the Cold War.

The failure of the Obama/Clinton reset with Russia should be viewed in terms of contradictory U.S. policies that tried to punish Russia for belligerent behavior while simultaneously trying to engage it as a partner to advance other U.S. policy goals.

RUSSIA'S UKRAINE INTERVENTION MET BY U.S. EMPTY THREATS

After pro-Russian President Viktor Yanukovich was ousted as a result of mass demonstrations in February 2014, Russia engaged in a series of efforts to intervene in Ukraine to undermine the new pro-Western government and advance Russian interests. This intervention included backing pro-Russian separatist forces and firing into Ukrainian territory from Russia. Pro-Russian Ukrainian rebels seized and continue to control two Ukrainian provinces: Donetsk and Luhansk. Although Russia denies its troops crossed the border into Ukraine, some Russian troops without insignia are believed to have entered Ukraine to fight alongside Ukrainian separatists and Ukrainian authorities captured several Russian troops on their soil.

On February 27, 2014, masked Russian troops without insignia performed a precision operation to seize control of the Ukrainian province of Crimea. After Crimeans overwhelmingly voted to join Russia in a March 16, 2014 referendum, Moscow annexed Crimea on March 18. The West rejected the referendum as illegitimate. (Roger Robinson explains in his chapter to this book his assessment that Crimea Black Sea energy deposits were a prime factor in Russia's annexation of Crimea.)

President Obama and Secretary Kerry warned that Russia would pay a price for its actions in Ukraine and made high-minded speeches demanding that it withdraw. Obama said in a March 2014 press conference "Russia is a regional power that is threatening some of its immediate neighbors — not out of strength but out of weakness." Secretary Kerry warned Putin in March 2014 that "all options were on the table" concerning a U.S. response and that Russian annexing Crimea would "close any available space for diplomacy." Kerry also chided Putin with a preposterous statement during a March 2, 2014 *Face the Nation* interview that "You just don't in the 21st century behave in 19th century fashion by invading another country on completely trumped up pretext."[5]

Some Obama officials and their supporters tried to defend the Obama administration's response to Russia's meddling in Ukraine by claiming it was no different than the Bush administration's response when Russia invaded Georgia in 2008. Brookings Foundation Senior Fellow Steven Pifer made this case in a March 2014 *Politico* op-ed titled "George W. Bush Was Tough on Russia? Give Me a Break."[6]

Pifer argued it is unfair for Obama's political opponents to criticize the president's failure to convince Russia to cease interfering in Ukraine or reverse its annexation of Crimea because the Bush administration employed similar policies in 2008 when Russia sent troops into Georgia and occupied the breakaway Georgian region of South Ossetia and also was unsuccessful.

Pifer wrote that like the Obama administration, the Bush administration ruled out military options in response to Russia's invasion of Georgia and had few good levers to influence the Kremlin due to "the deterioration in U.S.-Russian relations over the previous five years." Pifer also disputed claims by Bush officials that by airlifting Georgian troops from Afghanistan to Georgia during the conflict and sending U.S. warships to the Black Sea, the Bush administration prevented Russia from overthrowing Georgia's democratically elected government.

Although Pifer identified important factors similar to both cases, he omitted several key differences.

It is possible that a perception of a weaker Bush administration at the end of President Bush's second term in 2008 affected Putin's decision to invade Georgia. Also, similar to the Obama administration during the Ukraine crisis, Bush officials decided not to send military aid or U.S. troops to Georgia because they understood that Putin sees Russia as the protector of ethnic Russians living in these countries and considers them as part of a Russian sphere of influence.[7]

However, while the Bush administration condemned the 2008 Russian intervention in Georgia, it did not impose sanctions or issue ultimatums. Its response was stern and measured. This was because Bush officials realized the limits of their policy to reverse Russia's intervention and did not make demands of Russian leaders that they knew the U.S. would not back up. Senior Bush officials also understood that as bad as Russia's invasion of Georgia was, Washington needed to maintain a working relationship with Moscow.

This was not the case for the Obama administration. President Obama and Secretary Kerry mistakenly thought they could threaten and use sanctions to force Putin to reverse the 2014 Ukraine intervention and had no follow-up plan if Putin rejected their ultimatums. They had no understanding of the damage that could be done to American credibility – with Russia and around the world – if Putin disregarded their ultimatums as empty rhetoric. This lack of foresight contributed to Putin's disregard for the Obama administration and encouraged Russia to engage in more destabilizing and belligerent behavior in the belief that there would be no serious response from the United States.

Putin ignored U.S. ultimatums and sanctions over his meddling in Ukraine because he correctly predicted there was no chance the United States would send troops or arms to Ukraine. Putin knew the U.S. and its European allies would do nothing to defend Ukraine other than make empty threats and impose economic sanctions which he planned to ignore.

For these reasons, Russia never ended its meddling in Ukraine and the violence remained at a high level in 2014 and 2015.

Putin also was not cowed by U.S. demands to withdraw from Ukraine because he knew President Obama needed Russia's support on other international issues that Mr. Obama considered more important.

HOW THE IRAN NUCLEAR DEAL AFFECTED U.S./RUSSIA RELATIONS

While the Obama administration was sanctioning Russia and issuing ultimatums over its intervention in Ukraine, it was simultaneously seeking Russia's support for President Obama's most important foreign policy priority: a nuclear agreement with Iran. This agreement, which was announced in July 2015, was initially crafted in bilateral talks between the United States and Iran, and through P-5+1 talks (the United States, Russia, China, France, the United Kingdom and Germany) with Iran in 2012 and 2013. However, the formal negotiations in 2014 and 2015 required close U.S. coordination with Russian diplomats.

The Obama administration had no choice but to engage Russia in the Iran negotiations since Russia is a permanent member of the UN Security Council and has had a reasonably close relationship with Tehran.

Russian officials probably relished the irony of the Obama administration's attempting to work with them on Iran while also trying to punish Russia over Ukraine. This awkward situation provided several opportunities for the Kremlin to exploit in order to undermine American interests and advance Russian interests.

Russia has a history of manipulating American diplomacy on the Iran nuclear program that predates the Obama administration. The Clinton administration tried unsuccessfully to prevent Russia from providing nuclear technology to Iran – supposedly for peaceful purposes – and to halt its work to build Iran's Bushehr nuclear reactor.

The Bush administration tried to convince Russia to cease construction of the Bushehr reactor after evidence began to mount starting in 2002 that Iran had a covert nuclear weapons program. Russia refused and, along with China, undermined Bush administration efforts to pass Security Council resolutions sanctioning Iran over this program. Russia signed an agreement to provide nuclear fuel rods to operate this reactor but did not agree to delivery until after a controversial U.S. National Intelligence Estimate (NIE) was issued in November 2007 which concluded that Iran's nuclear program was halted in 2003. Although International Atomic Energy Agency reports[8] in 2015 proved this NIE was inaccurate – and Russia must have known this in 2007 – Russian officials probably used this report as an excuse to move forward with the Bushehr deal. More importantly, Russia most likely went forward with this deal because the second term Bush administration was seen as much weaker than the first term and Moscow knew Bush's Iran policy was being undermined by American intelligence agencies.

This behavior by Russia continued – and worsened – during the Obama years. Russia continued to work with China to weaken Security Council resolutions against Iran for covert nuclear weapons work. Putin tried to build ties to the virulently anti-American Iranian President Mahmoud Ahmadinejad, elected in 2005, and convince Ahmadinejad to let Russia enrich uranium and produce fuel rods for Iran's nuclear program. Although Iran did agree to let Russia produce fuel rods for Bushehr and send the spent rods back to Russia for disposal, Ahmadinejad refused to give up Iran's uranium enrichment program.

In 2014, Russia signed an agreement with Iran to build eight nuclear reactors. This deal raised concerns in the West since the Iran nuclear talks were still underway and their outcome was uncertain.

In 2007, Iran signed a contract with Russia to buy S-300 surface-to-air missiles, one of the most advanced systems of its type. This contract caused tension between the two countries because Moscow refused to deliver the missiles due to pressure by the Bush and Obama administrations as well as Iran's failure to pay.

Russia agreed to go forward with the S-300 deal in April 2015 after the announcement of an outline of the Iran nuclear deal. It began delivery of the missiles in April 2016. Iran is using the S-300s to protect its Fordow uranium enrichment site from U.S. and Israeli airstrikes. Why did Russia proceed with the S-300 deal despite the nuclear agreement which should have negated Iran's need for these missiles? Probably because Russia hoped to take advantage of what many believed would be significant new trade opportunities with Iran after UN, U.S. and EU sanction were lifted in the wake of the nuclear agreement. Moscow didn't care that Iran's continued interest in the S-300s indicated it could withdraw from the nuclear agreement in the near future because Russia only went along with the nuclear talks to advance its interests (especially trade deals with Iran) and to work with Tehran to undermine the United States. Russian officials probably share the view of many U.S. experts that although President Obama considers the 2015 nuclear deal with Iran one of his most important achievements, the deal is actually a very weak agreement that does not stop Iran's pursuit of nuclear weapons and will allow Iran to develop an industrial-scale nuclear weapons program in 10 to 15 years.[9]

IRAN DEAL EMBOLDENS RUSSIA IN SYRIA

Russia's meddling in the Syrian crisis is a direct result of the Iran nuclear talks, the Obama administration's policy of retreat in the Middle East, and an overall perception of U.S. weakness under the Obama administration.

Syria has long been a close ally and client state of the Soviet Union and Russia. Syria is strategically important to Russia because of the Russian naval facility in Tartus, Syria, Russia's only naval facility in the Mediterranean and the only remaining military facility outside the former Soviet Union. The Arab Spring uprising of 2011 greatly concerned Russian leaders because it threatened to replace Syrian President Bashar al-Assad – who like his father and predecessor President Hafez al-Assad had close relations with Moscow – with a new government run by Assad's political opponents who might terminate that relationship.

Although the Russian government has participated in various peace initiatives since 2011 to resolve the Syrian civil war, it has staunchly supported President Assad and provided him with a steady flow of military assistance, including artillery and tanks.

A key development in the Syria story occurred in August 2013 when Syria violated a "red line" that President Obama declared a year earlier in which he said the United States would use military force if Syria used chemical weapons against his own people.[10]

By early September 2013, pressure was growing on President Obama to take military action against the Assad regime for violating his red line on chemical weapons use. At the same time, Obama's bid to win congressional support for an attack on Syria appeared to be on the verge of a major defeat. Obama didn't want to take action without a congressional buy-in. Congress did not trust Obama to act.

The situation dramatically shifted on September 9 when Secretary of John Kerry made an offhand comment at a press conference in London that Assad could avoid a U.S. assault by giving up "every single bit of his chemical weapons to the international community in the next week." Russia immediately jumped on Kerry's statement when Foreign Minister Sergey Lavrov said Moscow would urge Syria to place its chemical weapons under international control. The Assad government quickly endorsed the Russian proposal.

Although I doubt President Obama would ever have approved a U.S. attack on Syria, U.S. and European forces were preparing an attack. The United States sent five Navy destroyers to the eastern Mediterranean. The UK was planning to join a possible attack on Syria from its airbases in Cyprus and from submarine-based missiles. The French government planned to join an attack on Syria but said little about its plans. French fighters might have attacked Syria from bases in the UAE.

Realizing that an attack against Syria might be imminent, Russia seized on Kerry's comment not just to block an attack but to avoid a diplomatic agreement that would punish the Assad regime for chemical weapons use and impose new steps to revolve the Syrian conflict. While this outcome was praised by most observers at the time (especially Obama officials since it got them out of a policy quandary), it significantly eased international pressure on Assad over his bloody campaign against the Syrian rebels.

Wall Street Journal writer Jay Solomon told MSNBC in August 2016 about another factor that may have caused President Obama to not back up his red line on Syrian CW use and agree to the compromise proposed by Russian Foreign Minister Lavrov.[11] According to Solomon, Iran threatened with withdraw from the nuclear talks if the U.S. or its allies attacked the Assad regime. Based on other major U.S. concessions to Iran to negotiate the nuclear agreement and other experts[12] who share Solomon's view, I believe he is probably right.

Solomon's claim also is plausible because the Obama administration was engaged in discussions about Iraq and Syria with Iran and Russia on the sidelines of the Iran nuclear talks. Moreover, according to the *Wall Street Journal*, in October 2014 President Obama sent a secret message to Iranian Supreme Leader Khamenei on how the United States and Iran might work together fighting ISIS in Iraq and Syria if a nuclear agreement could be reached.[13] This letter was extraordinary since it reportedly said that U.S. military operations in Syria and Iraq are not aimed at weakening Iran or its allies, including the Assad regime in Syria. This gave a green light to Iran to expand its role in Iraq and Syria and probably further angered America's allies about Obama's Middle East policy.

Iranian officials probably regarded U.S. offers during the nuclear talks to work with them on Iraq and Syria as an incredible windfall that would allow them to advance their goals of increasing Iranian power and influence in the region with the blessing, if not the assistance of, the United States.

After the nuclear agreement was announced in July 2015, Russian and Iranian support to the Assad regime increased significantly. Iran began to send ground troops to Syria for the first time in October 2015 and stepped up its arms shipments. Russia stunned the world when it sent fighters to Syria and began conducting airstrikes on September 30, 2015. While Russia claims these airstrikes only target terrorists, many have attacked rebel groups opposed to the Assad regime – including some backed by the United States – and have provided air support for Iranian troops.

In response to the Russian airstrikes, President Obama warned the Russian government:

> "An attempt by Russia and Iran to prop up Assad and try to pacify the population is just going to get them stuck in a quagmire and it won't work. And they will be there for a while if they don't take a different course."

Like similar warnings by Obama officials to Russia over the Ukraine crisis, Obama administration critics lambasted the president's statement as feckless. The Russian government ignored it.

Russia's stepped-up military support to Syria in the fall of 2015 changed the direction of the Syrian civil war. Moscow rescued the Assad regime at a time when experts were predicting the regime could collapse or Assad could be forced to step down. Through their increased military support, Iran and Russia propped up the Assad government to such an extent that there is no longer a reasonable prospect of removing Assad from power. As a result, the Obama administration was forced to drop its previous demand that Assad step down as part of a peace settlement. Russia's military support over the last year also helped the Assad regime recapture territory. This included airstrikes in support of the Syrian army's assault on the rebel-held town of Aleppo which resulted in a major humanitarian crisis. As Mark Schneider explains later in this book, Russia also has deployed powerful S-300 and S-400 surface to air missiles that gives it the ability to defend the Assad regime from air attacks in almost all of Syria.

By the fall of 2016, it was obvious that Russia's increased military support to the Assad regime had boosted Russian influence and credibility in the Middle East at America's expense. Russia did not get caught up in the quagmire President Obama had predicted. Instead, after successfully bolstering the Assad regime, Putin announced in April 2016 that Russia would withdraw the "main part" of its forces from Syria.

Russian diplomats have participated in various multilateral and bilateral efforts to bring about peace agreements and cease-fires in the Syrian crisis. A "partial" cease-fire was agreed to in February 2016 that lasted until July. Attacks by and against terrorist groups were not barred by this cease-fire. The Assad regime repeatedly violated the cease-fire. Although Moscow complained about cease-fire violations by rebel groups, Russia also was accused of violating the agreement by conducting airstrikes against rebel groups it claimed were terrorists.

The United States and Russia began a new round of diplomacy in August 2016 after the February 2016 agreement broke down. This resulted in a new cease-fire agreement that went into effect on September 12, 2016. This was an unusual agreement which held that if the cease-fire held for seven days, Russia and the United States would begin military coordination to target al-Qaeda affiliate Jabhat Fateh Al-Sham, previously known as the al-Nusra Front. U.S. defense and intelligence officials objected to this agreement because they opposed any military collaboration with Russia in Syria and worried that it would require sharing U.S. intelligence with Russia.

Russian officials must have been delighted when Secretary Kerry said on September 12 that the new U.S.-Russia agreement could permit the Syrian military to launch new airstrikes against al-Qaeda-linked militants. Kerry probably misspoke and the State Department quickly clarified that the United States had not agreed to this.

The September 2016 cease-fire agreement only lasted two weeks because Russian and Syrian forces violated it by intensifying their assault on Aleppo. Russia denied violating the cease-fire and blamed anti-regime Syrian rebels.

On September 28, 2016, Secretary Kerry condemned Syrian and Russian violations of the cease-fire and said the United States would halt talks with Russia on the war in Syria and drop the plan for military cooperation unless the Russian and Syrian militaries stopped bombing Aleppo. However, Kerry did not explain what steps the United States would take if Russia ignored his warning.

Russian officials rejected Kerry's warning by claiming "the whole opposition ostensibly fighting a civil war in Syria is a U.S.-controlled terrorist international" and accusing the United States of preparing to use terrorism against Russia.

Congressional critics of the Obama administration fiercely condemned Kerry's response as another feckless declaration by the Obama administration. Senators John McCain and Lindsey Graham said in a statement ridiculing Kerry:

> Finally, a real power move in American diplomacy. Secretary of State John 'Not Delusional' Kerry has made the one threat the Russians feared most – the suspension of U.S.-Russia bilateral talks about Syria. No more lakeside tête-à-têtes at five-star hotels in Geneva. No more joint press conferences in Moscow. We can only imagine that having heard the news, Vladimir Putin has called off his bear hunt and is rushing back to the Kremlin to call off Russian airstrikes on hospitals, schools, and humanitarian aid convoys around Aleppo. After all, butchering the Syrian people to save the Assad regime is an important Russian goal. But not if it comes at the unthinkable price of dialogue with Secretary Kerry.[14]

Although Russia ignored Kerry's warning, it did announce a unilateral cease-fire in Aleppo on October 21, 2016. This was expected to be a short-lived humanitarian pause in the fighting that would not improve the chances for peace.

By contrast, the French approach to Russia's intervention in Syria has been more principled, although still ineffective. On October 11, 2016, French Foreign Minister Jean-Marc Ayrault announced that France was exploring how the

International Criminal Court could begin an investigation of possible war crimes by Russian and Syrian forces in Aleppo. That same day, French President François Hollande said if Putin visited France, he would only meet with him to discuss the Syria situation and would not participate in a scheduled visit by Putin to inaugurate a new Russian Orthodox cathedral in Paris. Putin responded by cancelling his trip in what CNN termed a snub to French President Hollande.[15]

Meanwhile, a fleet of Russian warships and fighter jets, including the flagship aircraft carrier *Admiral Kuznetsov*, entered the English Channel on October 21, 2016 en route to the Mediterranean to conduct attacks in Syria. Peter Felstead, editor of *Jane's Defence Weekly*, told CNN he believed Russia sent this flotilla "as a show of force and a show of capabilities."[16]

The bottom line on events surrounding Ukraine, Syria and Iran as they relate to Russia during the Obama administration: Russia's behavior worsened and became more belligerent as the global perception of the Obama administration's weakness and indecisiveness grew. This belligerence accelerated in 2015 and 2016 due to the widespread view that Obama's Middle East policies were an utter failure and Obama officials were clueless on how to fix them.

OTHER WAYS THE OBAMA RUSSIA RESET FAILED

Destabilizing and anti-American Russian policies worsened in other areas over the last eight years due to the weakness of the Obama administration. Mark Schneider and Daniel Gouré explain in this book Russian efforts to rebuild its military and improve and expand its missile and nuclear arsenals. Kevin Freeman discusses how Russia expanded economic warfare against the United States, including by collaborating with China to end the use of the U.S. dollar as a global reserve currency. Michael Waller discusses Russia's growing information warfare efforts that include RT, an international cable channel that churns out anti-American propaganda.

I would add to these analyses a sharp increase in Russian intelligence operations against the United States, both cyber warfare and traditional intelligence operations using human agents. I strongly believe former NSA technician Edward Snowden was a recruited Russian agent before he began stealing U.S. secrets and leaking them to the news media. I fear there are more Snowdens in the U.S. government recruited due to Putin's efforts to reinvigorate Russian intelligence agencies and use them for new, aggressive operations against the United States.

CONCLUSION

Americans now know that the weakness and naiveté of the Obama administration, its foreign policy incompetence, and the power vacuums caused by President Obama's failure to lead on the world stage resulted in huge costs. When a U.S. president repeatedly issues worthless ultimatums and empty threats and draws red lines he fails to enforce, he undermines America's credibility in the eyes of our enemies as well as our friends.

These factors greatly exacerbated instability in the Middle East. They led to the birth of ISIS. They also emboldened America's enemies and adversaries across the globe.

The instances of Russia disrespecting America at the beginning of this chapter are symptoms of President Obama's disastrous foreign policy. They reflect how a Russian autocrat with a KGB/Soviet era mindset successfully exploited U.S. weakness to advance his goal of regaining for Russia some of the power and influence of the Soviet Union at America's expense. Putin has used American weakness to make progress toward his goal of drastically changing the current world order by ending the political, economic and military dominance of the United States.

The damage done by Putin's efforts to American security, as you will read elsewhere in this book, is profound and growing. Reversing this damage will be a herculean task, and could take many years. Most importantly, it will take principled and competent American leadership.

Russia's Goals and Objectives in Syria

By Stephen Blank

By midsummer 2016, Moscow had not only prevailed in Syria but was also driving U.S. Syria policy.[17] Russia also had forced Turkey to cooperate with it and acknowledge (at least at the time) Bashar Assad's continuation in power as a condition of rapprochement with Ankara.[18] Yet few – if any – analyses showed interest in Moscow's goals, not only for Syria but for the broader Middle East. Putin's successes now allow him to advance broader regional interests to formalize its military presence in Syria while riding roughshod over U.S. and Turkish policies.[19]

Few writers have considered Russia's broader, regional, and global, objectives beyond the notion that Moscow may be using Syria to extricate itself from the isolation generated by its invasion of Ukraine. Russians, however, openly concede that insight. Sergei Karaganov, a prominent Russian foreign policy analyst, admitted that, "Syria diverts everyone's attention from Ukraine and thus moves our relations with the West to another level."[20] Another correct but insufficiently explanatory objective is that Putin intervened primarily to show that Russia as a great power can act independently and force the world to take its behavior and interests seriously. Two other prominent analysts, Nadezhda Arbatova and Alexander Dynkin write that

> The main goal of Russia's involvement is to show that Moscow's assistance may play a crucial role in the settlement of major issues, such as the Syrian conflict and international terrorism, and to underline the point that the Islamic State (also known as ISIS or ISIL) is the greatest threat the world faces. Any improvement in Russia-West relations through cooperation on such issues would increase the chances of a lasting peace in Ukraine.[21]

While both these explanations certainly are part of the answer, they are incomplete. In Syria, Moscow pursues long-standing domestic, regional, global, military, and political interests. The military goals can be divided into three categories: strategic, operational, and tactical. For example, one clear tactical objective *is* the desire to use Syria as a testing ground for new weapons and capabilities to make sure they work and to display them to Western audiences.[22] Indeed, many reports claim that Russian weapons used in Syria impress potential customers while Russia avidly cites Syria as a testimonial for its weapons.[23] Putin has intimated that one goal of the operation was to test and display capabilities and certainly certain operations, e.g. firing Kalibr' cruise missiles from Caspian Sea-based frigates on Putin's birthday in 2015 aim to broadcast Russian capabilities to both potential buyers and adversaries alike.[24]

Finally, some Russian objectives have either become more important or emerged as a result of the fighting, particularly the determination to humiliate Turkey after it shot down a Russian fighter, and the desire to aggravate European disunity by a bombing campaign that would generate mass flight of refugees to an overburdened Europe.[25] An August 2016 Putin-Erdogan summit illustrated the former point as Putin will only lift economic sanctions gradually upon Turkey to force it to change its policies.[26] Since political objectives often evolve with the course of combat operations, this is not surprising. But it is a sign of many analysts' strategic failings that they claim that such adaptations signify Russian failure rather than realizing that they indicate an unexpected flexibility and determination, i.e. attributes of strength, not weakness.

RUSSIAN OBJECTIVES

As many writers and the Russian government have noted, internal and external security and the means of achieving them are fused in Putin's Russia. Since the National Security Strategy of 2009, virtually all areas of Russian social and cultural life have been "securitized."[27] As the state grows increasingly more concerned about foreign ideas and influences, it has assumed ever more responsibility for steering the entire socio-economic-cultural and political lives of the Russian people.

Concurrently, there is an ongoing mobilization of the entire Russian state for purposes of permanent, albeit mainly non-military, conflict with foreign governments.[28] This securitization and mobilization paradigm provides the context for understanding Moscow's Syrian gambit. As Moscow has frequently claimed, its perspective on the Middle East is closely tied to threats to the state's domestic stability, particularly threats from Islamic terrorism.[29]

This commingling of internal and external threats is part of the officially sanctioned approach to national security and foreign policy in Putin's Russia. As the 2008 Foreign Policy Concept of the Russian Federation states: "Differences between domestic and external means of ensuring national interests and security are gradually disappearing. In this context, our foreign policy becomes one of major instruments of the steady national development."[30]

Several scholars have concluded that since the Russian public is in favor of asserting Russia's great power standing, Putin must hold such a view. This sentiment grips Russian elites and society even without the government's systematic saturation of the media on this point. In 2000, John Loewenhardt of the Netherlands Institute of International Relations reported

> In one of our interviews a former member of the Presidential Administration said that the perception of Russia as a great power "is a basic element of the self-perception of high bureaucrats." If a political leader were to behave as if Russia was no longer a great power, there would be "a deeply rooted emotional reaction in the population."[31]

Russian leaders have repeatedly echoed the sentiment that Russia is an inherent great power that must act independently of the international system. For example, upon becoming Foreign Minister in 1996 Yevgeny Primakov stated

> Russia's foreign policy cannot be the foreign policy of a second-rate state. We must pursue the foreign policy of a great state. The world is moving toward a multipolar system. In these conditions we must pursue a diversified course oriented toward the development of relations with everyone, and at the same time, in my view, we should not align ourselves with any individual pole. Precisely because Russia itself will be one of the poles, the "leader-led" configuration is not acceptable to us.[32]

Other writers have similarly observed that Putin's conduct of foreign policy is a critical aspect of the restoration of both the state and Russia's great power standing abroad, Putin's two key objectives throughout his rule. Thus, actions validating Russia as an independent, sovereign, great, power evoke strong public support. As Dr. Vitaly Kozyrev explained in a 2010 paper,

> Many decisions concerning security issues are related to the factor of *legitimacy of the ruling elite*, rather than the correlation between Russia's power and capabilities. Being unable to secure required conditions for a qualitative breakthrough toward an effective economic model and relying increasingly on natural resources for economic growth, the governing groups constantly feel a danger of social unrest and the pressure from competing influential political and business circles.[33]

This understanding becomes particularly important because the government explicitly regards its domestic security as unstable and the state as having failed to achieve the "necessary level of public security."[34] And this instability is traceable, in no small measure, to Islamic terrorism and criminality.[35] Therefore, preventing the spread of terrorism beyond the North Caucasus and ultimately eliminating it are major state priorities. Russian leaders' endless reiterations that they intervened in Syria to prevent terrorists from returning home clearly has a basis in Russian policy and implicitly underscores the connection from internal to external security even if Moscow helped terrorists move to Syria to reduce terrorism in the North Caucasus.[36]

Domestic instability clearly impedes realization of restoring Russia's acknowledged great power status, not only in the former Soviet sphere but beyond it, particularly in the Middle East, an area that Moscow still maintains is close to its borders despite the Soviet collapse in 1991. Therefore Moscow's actions in Syria strongly represent the much broader phenomenon of commingling of both internal and external means of ensuring security in order to realize this great power program. According to Luke Chambers, a foreign affairs analyst for the UK Conservative Party,

> Endogenous and exogenous behavior and processes in the last decade relating to Russia should not be viewed as discrete: instead there is analytical value in evaluating the Kremlin's domestic and foreign agendas as part of a wider, unitary strategy to restore Russia's role as a global actor. The design pursued domestically exerts a strong influence on foreign policy; accordingly, the long-term goals of Russian foreign policy are lodged within the Russian state as well as without.[37]

Imperialism and power projection abroad, most recently seen in Ukraine and Syria, are intrinsic to the great power project and inherent in the structure and nature of the Russian state.[38] Indeed, the long-standing desire to restore Russia to its previous Cold War prominence in the Middle East at Washington's expense dovetailed in the wake of the "Arab Spring" in 2011. As Prime Minister, Putin very quickly expressed fear that the revolts in Tunisia, Egypt, and Libya would "inevitably" engender greater violence in the North Caucasus.[39] Similarly, then-President Medvedev openly expressed the Kremlin's belief that these insurgencies were direct result of a foreign conspiracy against Russia.[40] Since then, this justification for acting in the Middle East has continued uninterrupted and Russian officials continually claim that their bombing raids are eliminating the terrorists. Evidently, for Moscow all opposition to Russian allies and/or interests is inherently terrorist in nature and justifies virtually any response.

Additionally, there are several other important domestic goals that a short, victorious war in Syria might serve. Dmitiri Trenin, Director of the Moscow office of the Carnegie Endowment, states that an "expanding Russian presence in the region's arms, nuclear, oil and gas, food, and other markets," will reward key interest groups in

Putin's ruling "coalition," attracting foreign investments from Gulf regimes, and supporting energy prices by coordinating policies with the principal Gulf oil and gas producers.[41] Moscow's efforts to acquire such loans and promote such coordination, even if they have hitherto failed and reveal thereby the limits of Russian capabilities, underscore the breadth of its interests and the objectives that successes in Syria offer it.[42]

Economist Vladislav Inozemstsev observed that because Putin's regime cannot deliver tangible economic progress, it must compensate by forming a new political consensus around the obsession with great power status and an accompanying program of foreign policy adventurism.[43] Inozemstsev also adds that there was a necessity for the Kremlin to find a new propaganda theme. Support was declining for the invasion of Ukraine by mid-2015, and a new avenue was needed for stimulating the great power obsession.[44] Lastly, Inozemstev emphasizes the need to obtain arms export markets, enhance prestige for the military, and keep the defense industrial sector fully employed to prevent discontent.[45]

Adam Garfinkle, editor of *The American Interest*, echoes Inozemstev's argument about the desirability of increasing arms sales and enriching that sector to sustain it.[46] Key lobbies like arms sales and energy will benefit from contracts relating to Syria.[47] These views imply that Syria is not the last manifestation of Russian adventurism, as too many stakeholders stand to gain from similar policies in the future. And if we add to those views a key lesson of this campaign that force works, then forestalling the next Syria becomes a critical task for Western governments.

Therefore it is quite unlikely that Putin can renounce the obsession with great power status. If Moscow reined in its ambitions to a more manageable size and refrained from imperialistic behavior abroad, the state might collapse.[48] Absent reform, which will not occur, foreign adventures are the only option left to him to maximize his popularity, legitimacy and domestic power. Absent bread, only circuses are left.

Adventures like Syria and Ukraine are essential to perpetuating Putin's Russia and defending energy and arms sale sectors of the state-controlled economy. Examination of Russian policies in the Middle East quickly reveals the saliency and linkages between arms sales and major energy deals.[49] Moreover, it appears that the steady increase of arms transfers to Syria in 2011-13 was linked in Putin's mind to preventing another "color revolution" in Ukraine. In other words, the successful and stealthy employment of the navy and other organs to increase arms supplies to Syria helped convince Putin to invade Ukraine as did the linkages between preventing the triumph of revolutions in other areas of importance to Moscow.[50]

These energy and arms sales interests along with strategic considerations may become more important given Russia's current economic crisis. Whereas Russia's energy deals with Middle Eastern producers aim at enhancing Russian leverage on energy supplies to Europe which are themselves Russian political weapons, energy deals and arms sales enhance Moscow's regional and overall foreign policy standing, obtain profit for key elites, obtain hard currency, and block American interests. In Libya and Egypt alone, Moscow lost $4 billion in arms sales due to revolutions.[51] A 2007 classified diplomatic cable by U.S. Ambassador to Russia William Burns disclosed by Wikileaks in 2014 captured the motives for Russian arms sales to Middle East states:

> A second factor driving the Russian arms export policy is the desire to enhance Russia's standing, as a "player" in areas where Russia has a strategic interest, likes the Middle East. Russian officials believe that building a defense relationship provides ingress and influence, and their terms are not constrained by conditionality. Exports to Syria and Iran are part of a broader strategy of distinguishing Russian policy from that of the United States, and strengthening Russian influence in international for a such as the Quartet or within the Security council. With respect to Syria, Russian officials believe that the Assad regime is better than the perceived alternative of instability or an Islamist government, and argue against a U.S. policy of isolation. Russia has concluded that its arms sales are too insignificant to threaten Israel, or to disturb growing Israeli-Russian diplomatic engagement, but sufficient to maintain "special" relations with Damascus. Likewise, arms sales to Iran are part of a deep and multilayered bilateral relationship that serves to distinguish Moscow from Washington, and to provide Russian officials with a bargaining chip both with the Ahmadinejad regime and its P5+ 1 partners. While, as a matter of practice, Russian arms sales have declined as international frustration has mounted over the Iranian regime, as a matter of policy, Russia does not support what it perceives as U.S. efforts to build an anti-Iranian coalition.[52]

Economic gains to the state, defense sector, and to officials who exploit their private and government positions are also critical to blocking American policies as Burns also explained in the 2007 cable leaked by Wikileaks

> A variety of factors drive Russian arms sales, but a compelling motivation is profit - both licit and illicit. It is an open secret that the Russian defense industry is an important trough at which senior officials feed, and weapons sales continue to enrich many.[53]

Beyond all these aforementioned interests, the Putin regime, at least since 2008, has steadily endeavored to impart a "civilizational" basis to its foreign policy and masquerades as the last bastion of Christian civilization and values against a decadent Europe. But in the Islamic world and with Muslim audiences it similarly masquerades as an Islamic state. This ideological posturing allows it to do business with any Arab country or Iran "with no questions asked"

> Russia accepts the semi-traditional nature of the post-Soviet Muslim regimes and is not obsessed with whether they are secular or not. Moscow is happy enough to recognize their "unique nature" and loudly proclaims its skepticism over the idea of applying a Western model to them that is alien to their identity. The notions of "particularities of national democracy" and the "need to preserve a specific civilization identity are music to the ears of Moscow politicians, busy promoting their own idea of "Russia's own development pathway" and their own variety of "sovereign democracy." Russia would have these regimes in a state of eternal transition, making it easier to deal with the local authorities and maintain its presence in the region.[54] According to Professor Roland Dannreuther:

In conclusion, there are four principal dimensions to Russian policy: (1) stabilizing the North Caucasus against the ideologies and activities of Islamic terrorism; (2) enhancing the legitimacy of Russia's current political order through displays of unconstrained "great power" behavior amidst a general mobilization of the state and society to a state of permanent expectation of conflict; (3) making private and state economic gains that accrue to elites from arms and energy deals in the Middle East, and (4) strengthening Russia's Middle Eastern position at Washington's expense.[55]

All these factors display signs of using foreign policy opportunities to entrench a particular dominating elite coalition in Russian policymaking. However, since the invasion of Ukraine, the threats to stability within Russia due to economic distress and state incapacity to alleviate it have grown along with its enmity towards the West by a considerable order of magnitude. Therefore we cannot explain the intervention in Syria only or primarily by domestic and economic considerations but equally by prominent geopolitical and strategic considerations. Domestic instability breeds an addiction to foreign policy adventurism that expresses itself in a necessity to keep taking ever bigger risks regardless of consequences. These considerations help place Russia in a permanent state of conflict or siege with its interlocutors where Putin must, due to his own interests, "seek the bubble reputation even in the mouth of the cannon." Thus Syria may not be the last of his provocations but just one in a series of escalating Russian provocations.

FOREIGN POLICY GOALS

Moscow's military operations also serve specific, identifiable, and long-standing regional and global foreign policy goals, including objectives pertaining to Ukraine and European security more broadly. Russia's current objectives in the Middle East apparently derive from Yevgeny Primakov's tenure as Foreign and Prime Minister from 1996 to 1999. In many ways Russian strategy towards the Middle East is essentially negative. It is haunted by the prospect of any foreign power getting a lasting foothold there and from there into the Commonwealth of Independent States (CIS). Therefore, it aims at preventing anyone else from stabilizing the area. As the historian Niall Ferguson observed, "Russia, thanks to its own extensive energy reserves, is the only power that has no vested interest in stability in the Middle East."[56] Russia has been able occasionally to obstruct or frustrate foreign policies of other governments, but until now it has failed spectacularly to create anything of a positive lasting nature abroad.

We can characterize the Kremlin's policy as strategic denial in economics, diplomacy, and military policy. Moscow discerns threats of varying intensity, but always of substance from *any* consolidated Western presence in Europe or in the Middle East, that would open the way to that presence in the CIS. Primakov long argued that it is essential for Russia and the Middle East that the United States not be the only regional hegemon.[58] In 1991, Primakov said that Middle Eastern leaders "consider it necessary that a united economic and military-strategic area of the USSR be preserved."

Primakov actually aimed to contrapose Russia everywhere as an antipode to the U.S. when he observed

> Yes, Russia is weakened. No, Russia cannot be compared with the Soviet Union, not even in terms of military potential. Nevertheless, everywhere one senses an interest in Russia's being present as an active participant in events, in Russia's attempting to balance the negative tendencies that could arise from a drive to establish a unipolar world.[57]

Thus Primakov sought a global standing for Russia where it would be equal to the United States in regard to regional security issues worldwide, not only the Middle East. Allegedly this would constitute a more 'democratic' system because Russia, as a permanent member of the UN Security Council, could veto Security Council resolutions endorsing any U.S. unilateral interventions.[58]

In the Middle East, Primakov counted on forces that resisted American hegemony and were looking to Russia to counter it; e.g. Iran, Saddam Hussein's Iraq, and Syria. According to Professor Alvin Rubinstein:

> They wanted a USSR presence in the Middle East because this would preserve the balance of power. Nobody wants some power to maintain a monopoly position there. These states understand that our country creates an area of stability in this region with its new policy of non-confrontation with anyone, a policy oriented toward searching for ways of making interests coincide with those of other countries.[59]

Primakov also argued that for Russia to succeed in the Middle East it had to oppose the U.S. and not surrender to its will.

> We explain our inadequate activity in the Near East by the fact that our efforts were aimed at evening our relations with the former cold war adversaries. But this was done without an understanding of the fact that, by not surrendering our positions in the region and even strengthening them, we would have paved the way to the normalization of relations. A shorter and more direct way.[60]

Other critical points of this approach to the Middle East beyond countering American power and influence was and remains developing relationships with key countries to create a functioning bloc or alliance of like-minded states against U.S. ambitions. This primarily focused on Iran despite Moscow's consistent opposition to its nuclearization. Nonetheless, what is key for Moscow is Iran's orientation to partnership with Russian aims on a host of regional security issues. Yeltsin advisor Andranik Migranyan stated in 1995 that

> In many areas Iran can be a good and strategic ally of Russia at [the] global level to check the hegemony of third parties and keep the balance of power. ...Russia will try to further cooperate with Iran as a big regional power. We will not let the West dictate to Russia how far it can go in its relations. Of course, we will try at the same time not to damage our relations with the West.[61]

Russia also clearly wanted and still wants to internationalize the issue of Gulf security, become a recognized guarantor of the area, either through the U.N. or through a regional alignment, and displace American primacy there.[62] Accordingly, Primakov supported the removal of foreign U.S. troops from the Gulf.[63] Iranian officials, too, also indicated an overt desire to arrive at a "division of responsibilities with Russia in regard to regional conflicts and energy issues."[64]

The ongoing continuity of those views remains quite visible. By 2014, Russian goals and capabilities in the Middle East had expanded. They included supporting the Assad regime against the Syrian rebels, even though military intervention had not yet occurred. More important than support for Assad whom Moscow at one time entreated to step down, this is a question of preserving his pro-Russian state even if it is reformed in some unspecified way.[65] Indeed, Putin reportedly told Assad in October 2015 "We won't let you lose." [66] But the key objective is not preserving Assad. Rather it is preserving his pro-Russian state system.[67]

By 2015, the insurgency threatened to destroy the Assad regime. Iran reportedly warned Putin of this in January 2015. Planning then began for an intervention, followed by a major snap-exercise in southern Russia in the spring of 2015 to rehearse for it. By the summer, a massive sea and airlift were underway. Russian military officials said "the drills were aimed at testing the readiness of the military to "manage coalition groups of troops in containing an international armed conflict." The Ministry of Defense additionally said that "Troops will simulate blocking and destroying illegal armed formations during joint special operations." Yet nobody in the West grasped what was happening.[68]

Beyond rescuing and stabilizing Assad's state (if not Assad himself) Moscow sought, and has gained, permanent naval and air bases in Syria and might even store nuclear weapons there.[69] Upon annexing Crimea, Moscow immediately accelerated the pre-existing large-scale modernization of the Black Sea Fleet to augment its overall naval capabilities, including a renewed permanent Mediterranean Squadron by 2016.[70] On February 26, 2014, Russian Defense Minister Sergei Shoigu announced talks with eight governments to establish a global network of airbases to extend the reach of Russia's long-range maritime and strategic aviation assets and increase Russia's global military presence.[71] Shoigu stated, "We are working actively with the Seychelles, Singapore, Algeria, Cyprus, Nicaragua, Venezuela, and even in some other countries. We are in talks and close to a result." Shoigu cited Russia's need for refueling bases near the equator and that "It is imperative that our navy has the opportunities for replenishment."[72] Since then the search for bases in Cuba and Vietnam, has, if anything become more overt.[73]

In May 2014, Deputy Defense Minister Anatoly Antonov announced that Russia is negotiating to establish support facilities in unspecified Middle Eastern countries, presumably Syria, Cyprus, and Egypt. Since then, Russia has acquired bases in Cyprus and Syria. Moscow also clearly desires naval base access to Alexandria, Egypt. In August 2014, responding to NATO's heightened naval presence in the Black Sea due to Ukrainian crisis, Shoigu demanded a new naval modernization plan to "improve the operational readiness of Russian naval forces in locations providing the greatest strategic threat."[74] In June 2014 Russian ships even deployed for the first time west of Sicily.[75] These moves show why dominating the Black Sea is critical for Russia's power projection into the Mediterranean and Middle East.[76]

However, Russia's Mediterranean Squadron may be as much a response to declining NATO deployments that created a strategic vacuum there, as it is a conscious strategy.[77] Since 2014, Moscow has reinforced the Black Sea Fleet to use it as a platform for denying NATO access to it, Ukraine, Russia, and the Caucasus and as a platform for power projection into the Mediterranean and Middle East.[78] Since intervening in Syria, Moscow has fortified the Squadron's missile, air defense, and submarine component to deny the area and access to it to NATO fleets in the Mediterranean. Indeed, the Russian fleet in Syria is busily constructing anti-access and area denial capabilities, e.g. land and sea-based air defenses, against NATO and other foreign militaries into the Eastern Mediterranean. This represents a clear sea denial strategy against NATO and other regional fleets just as in the Black Sea and other maritime theaters.[79] And by May 2016 U.S. intelligence confirmed that Moscow was building an army base at Palmyra.[80]

All these recent moves bespeak an enhanced regional power projection and political influence capabilities in the Levant. However, Moscow's goals were quite clear before 2015.

- Restoring the perception that Russia is a true great power that can and will block American initiatives, power and values, prevent Washington from unilaterally consolidating any regional geopolitical order, and force it to engage Moscow's interests and even its veto power through the UN upon US policies.
- Gaining great power status in Arab eyes and thus demonstrating its inherent and unconstrained ability to conduct a truly "independent" great power policy without Washington's approval.[81]
- By presenting a credible and vigorous alternative to Washington, Moscow aims to create a bloc of states aligned to it that opposes US positions on the Middle East, particularly Iran, Iraq, and Assad's Syria. This amounts to a pro-Shiite bloc against Sunni fundamentalism embodied by Saudi Arabia. The ultimate point is forcing the U.S. to act with Russia in the Middle East and not unilaterally, or in other terms to obtain not just equal standing with Washington but the ability to block its penchant for unilateral moves and establish a kind of condominium or concert of powers over future regional developments at Washington's

expense. Or as Foreign Minister Lavrov observed, "the Americans understand they can do nothing without Russia. They can no longer solve serious problems on their own".[82] Syria is merely one such example by which Moscow hopes to force Washington to treat it as a global equal.

- Parlaying Russian status in Syria into a demand for equal standing in an international Russo-American anti-terrorist coalition that will also induce the West to become "more reasonable" regarding Ukraine and Russian interests in Europe and Eurasia.
- Demonstrating at home and abroad reliability as an ally and staunch resolve to fight terrorism, while simultaneously posing as an exemplar of inter-civilizational understanding and the only true exemplar of universal religious values.
- Obtaining, through energy and arms deals, along with the judicious display of force, and sustained diplomacy, enduring leverage within if not over Middle Eastern governments that gives it a permanent base of influence upon their policies and erodes the credibility of Washington's Middle Eastern alliance system.
- Preserving Bashar Assad, or more likely his government's power over significant areas of Syria if not the entire state, but maintaining it in a "federalized" state to prevent future uprisings and also to ensure the predominance or at least the "blocking presence" of pro-Moscow elements so that the state will always be pro-Russian or at least susceptible to pro-Russian lobbies and unable to exit that situation.
- Humiliating Turkey and its plans to oust Assad and demonstrating that it cannot impose its will in Syria (or for that matter anywhere else) against Russian interests. Thus, forcing Turkey to follow a pro-Russian policy that actually curtails Turkey's large geopolitical ambitions and reaffirms its energy, economic, and hence strategic dependence upon Russia and not only in the Middle East.[83]
- Enhancing the regime's domestic standing as a successful exponent of Russia's great power interests and resolution in fighting terrorism while not letting itself be perceived as an enemy of Islam-a major consideration given its growing and large Muslim minority.[84]

As of today, Moscow has made considerable progress in all these areas with the help of a truly astonishing American strategic incompetence. Moscow has proven that war remains a method for states to actually achieve strategic interests. This realism may discomfit the Obama Administration and many analysts. But as John Adams said, "Facts are stubborn things."

Russian Nuclear Weapons, Strategic Defenses and Nuclear Arms Control Policy

By Mark B. Schneider

There are fundamental differences between U.S. and Russian nuclear strategy, nuclear modernization programs and arms control policy. While the U.S. is reducing its nuclear forces, in 2011 Russia's Defense Minister announced that Russia would increase its strategic nuclear forces.[85] In December 2012, the Director of National Intelligence's National Intelligence Council observed, "Reducing the role of nuclear weapons in US security strategy is a US objective, while Russia is pursuing new concepts and capabilities for expanding the role of nuclear weapons in its security strategy."[86] This stark difference is eroding our nuclear deterrent and increasing the risk of war. A 2016 report by the National Institute for Public Policy (NIPP) titled "Russian Strategy: Expansion, Crises, and Conflict" underscored, "Russian foreign military actions, defense initiatives, markedly expanded conventional and nuclear arms programs, internal repression, and egregious arms control non-compliance appear to be elements of an increasingly assertive and threatening agenda."[87]

RUSSIAN NUCLEAR STRATEGY AND THE RISK OF NUCLEAR WAR

According to Igor Ivanov, Russia's Foreign Minister under Yeltsin and Putin and Secretary of the Russian National Security Council under Putin, "The risk of confrontation with the use of nuclear weapons in Europe is higher than in the 1980s."[88] If so, the fundamental differences between U.S. and Russian foreign and nuclear weapons policies are responsible. The 2016 NIPP report cited above concluded, "Different elements of Russian policy and behavior typically are examined independently, as if they are unique and unrelated. The elements of contemporary Russian grand strategy under President Vladimir Putin, however, appear to be integrated and underlie much of Russia's defense and foreign policy behavior."[89] The problems we now face in deterring a Russian attack on NATO, which should be easy, reflect our unwillingness to assess Russian foreign and defense policy objectives realistically and to fund defense adequately, particularly nuclear deterrence programs. While Defense Department leaders recognize that Russia is an existential threat,[90] U.S. defense budget decisions don't reflect this reality.[91]

Noted Russian journalist Pavel Felgenhauer has characterized Western policy as "swinging between deterrence and appeasement." [92] He further noted, "Appeasement of authoritarian regimes like Russia's routinely fails because it is interpreted as a manifestation of weakness, which solicits more aggressive actions to obtain even more concessions."[93]

Since the end of the Cold War, U.S. forces most suitable for deterring Russia have generally not been modernized, have been reduced in number and, in some cases, have been scrapped. The average age of U.S. nuclear weapons is 27 years.[94] U.S. nuclear delivery vehicles have not been modernized for about 20 years and the projected future modernization is both distant and slow.[95] Russia is preparing to fight us and we are seriously preparing to fight only terrorists.

Since 2000, Russia has openly proclaimed that it reserves the right to introduce nuclear weapons into conventional war. [96] In October 2009, Russian National Security Council Secretary Sergei Patrushev said this included regional and local wars.[97] In December 2009, then-Commander of the Strategic Missile Troops Lieutenant General Andrey Shvaychenko remarked, "In a conventional war, they [the nuclear ICBMs] ensure that the opponent is forced to cease hostilities, on advantageous conditions for Russia, by means of single or multiple preventive strikes against the aggressors' most important facilities."[98] In December 2013, Deputy Prime Minister Dmitri Rogozin declared that if Russia is subject to a conventional attack, *"we will certainly resort to using nuclear weapons in certain situations to defend our territory and state interests."*[99] (Emphasis in the original). In September 2014, General of the Army (ret.) Yuri Baluyevskiy stated "conditions for pre-emptive nuclear strikes…is contained in classified policy documents." [100] In February 2015, Ilya Kramnik, military correspondent for state-run *RIA Novosti* until it was purged by Putin, wrote that the 2010 revision of Russia's military doctrine (still in effect) "further lowered" the threshold of "combat use" of nuclear weapons.[101]

Russia has practiced the first use of nuclear weapons in its theater war exercises against NATO and others since 1999 when simulated nuclear first use was officially announced.[102] Since then, there have been many reports of Russian nuclear first use in large theater exercises.[103] In January 2016, NATO's annual report stated, "Russia has conducted at least 18 large-scale snap exercises, some of which have involved more than 100,000 troops. These exercises include simulated nuclear attacks on NATO Allies (e.g., ZAPAD) and on partners (e.g. March 2013 simulated attacks on Sweden)..."[104] A 2015 Rand study concluded that Russia could militarily overrun the three NATO Baltic states capitals in 36 to 60 hours.[105] Putin has claimed that he can capture five NATO capitals by force in two days.[106] In 2014, he said that Russia could alone "strangle" all of NATO.[107] Lieutenant General Sir Adrian Bradshaw, Deputy Supreme Commander of NATO forces in Europe, has voiced concern about a Russian conventional attack on a weak NATO state backed by the threat of escalation to deter a NATO response.[108]

Russia is very optimistic about its ability to control escalation after nuclear weapons are used. Russia believes that Russian first use would "de-escalate" the conflict and result in a Russian victory.[109] In June 2015, U.S. Deputy Secretary of Defense Robert Work and then-Vice Chairman of the Joint Chiefs of Staff Admiral James Winnefeld observed, "Russian military doctrine includes what some have called an 'escalate to de-escalate' strategy – a strategy that purportedly seeks to de-escalate a conventional conflict through coercive threats, including limited nuclear use," a policy they categorized as "playing with fire."[110] In March 2016, Robert Scher, Assistant Secretary of Defense for Strategy, Plans and Capabilities, testified before the Congress that Russia has "adopted a pattern of reckless nuclear posturing and coercive threats. Russia remains in violation of the Intermediate-Range Nuclear Forces (INF) Treaty and remains unreceptive to the President's offer to negotiate further reductions in strategic nuclear weapons below the limits of the New START Treaty." He continued, "Russia's purported doctrine of nuclear escalation to de-escalate a conventional conflict amounts to a reckless gamble for which the odds are incalculable and the outcome could prove catastrophic."[111]

Russia has been making overt nuclear threats since 2007. Putin personally made several threats to target Russian missiles against U.S. friends and allies.[112] Indeed, in a February 2008 face-to-face meeting with the President of Poland, Putin said, "If it appears [missile defense in Europe], we will be forced to respond appropriately – we will have to retarget part of our systems against those missiles."[113] In 2008, General of the Army Yuri Baluyevskiy, then-Chief of the General Staff, stated that "for the protection of Russia and its allies, if necessary, the Armed Forces will be used, including preventively and with the use of nuclear weapons."[114] In 2008, Colonel General Nikolai Solovtsov, then-Commander of the Strategic Missile Troops, said "some of our ICBMs could be targeted at missile defense sites in Poland and the Czech Republic, and subsequently at other such facilities."[115] In 2009, Sergei Patrushev, Secretary of the Russian National Security Council, said that Russian nuclear policy "does not rule out a nuclear strike targeting a potential aggressor, including a preemptive strike, in situations critical to national security."[116] In March 2015, Russia's Ambassador to Denmark Mikhail Vanin made, perhaps, the most explicit of the nuclear targeting threats: "I don't think that Danes fully understand the consequence if Denmark joins the American-led missile defense shield. If they do, then Danish warships will be targets for Russian nuclear missiles."[117] In May 2016, Putin said that Poland will be in Russia's "cross hairs" and the Russian Defense Ministry declared Romania could be turned into "smoking ruins."[118]

Since the beginning of Russian aggression in Ukraine, a main focus of Russian nuclear threats has been on deterring a NATO counter attack.[119] In February 2016, Lieutenant General Ben Hodges, U.S. Army commander in Europe noted that "they [Russia] do talk a lot about using tactical nuclear weapons."[120] In July 2016, NATO Supreme Allied Commander Europe General Curtis M. Scaparrotti noted, "Russian doctrine states that tactical nuclear weapons may be used in a conventional response scenario."[121] General Bradshaw has also stated that the NATO rapid deployment force must be armed with the same weapons Russia has, that is, tactical nuclear weapons.[122] Unfortunately, this won't happen. These weapons have almost entirely been eliminated by NATO nations. With regard to the remaining gravity bombs, a 2009 NATO information publication proclaimed, "…NATO has radically reduced its reliance on nuclear forces.…Taking further advantage of the improved security environment, NATO has taken a number of steps to decrease the number and readiness levels of its dual-capable aircraft."[123]

Unlike the U.S., Russia is now introducing new nuclear capabilities, both strategic and tactical. A declassified August 2000 CIA report stated that there were "powerful advocates" for the development of very low-yield nuclear weapons in the Russian military and the Atomic Energy Ministry and the range of applications for sub-kiloton nuclear weapons "could include artillery, air-to-air missiles, ABM weapons, anti-satellite weapons, or multiple rocket launchers against tanks or massed troops."[124] In 2009, the bipartisan U.S. Strategic Commission report said Russia was developing "low-yield tactical nuclear weapons including an earth penetrator."[125] In May 2014, in a major nuclear exercise presided over by Putin, Russia announced the launch of several tactical nuclear-capable missiles and bombardment rockets.[126] According to one NATO diplomat, "What worries us most in this strategy is the modernization of the Russian nuclear forces, the increase in the level of training of those forces and the possible combination between conventional actions and the use of nuclear forces, including possibly in the framework of a hybrid war."[127]

RUSSIAN STRATEGIC NUCLEAR MODERNIZATION

There is a fundamental difference between U.S. and Russian strategic nuclear modernization programs. U.S. modernization will begin in the late 2020s, is partial and involves four systems through 2040, of which only two are now under contract. Every year since 1997, Russia has introduced modernized strategic nuclear strike capability, improving its deterrent and war fighting capability in a serious way. Deployed Russian forces are likely to increase even if we assume compliance with New START, reaching about 3,000 actual deployed warheads by about 2030.[128] A few of the new Russian systems are dual-capable (i.e., conventional and nuclear). Their announced programs include over 20 new or modernized strategic delivery systems, most of which are clearly new (i.e., post-Cold War designs). They are:[129]

- A new road-mobile and silo-based Topol-M Variant 2 (SS-27 Mod 1) ICBM.
- A new RS-24/Yars/SS-27 Mod 2 derivative with a Multiple Independently-targetable Re-entry Vehicle (MIRV) payload.
- Improved versions of the Soviet legacy SS-N-23 SLBM called the Sineva and the Liner with many more warheads.
- A new six warhead Bulava-30 SLBM being deployed on two types of the new Borey class submarine.
- A program to give the legacy SS-19 ICBM a hypersonic glider vehicle.
- Modernization of Blackjack (Tu-160) and Bear (Tu-95) heavy bombers which are armed with: 1) a new stealthy long-range strategic nuclear cruise missile designated the KH-102; and 2) the new stealthy long-range KH-101 cruise missile which, in December 2015, President Putin revealed "can be equipped either with conventional or special nuclear warheads."
- A program to produce at least 50 more of an improved version of the Tu-160 heavy bomber.

- Development and deployment by 2023-2025 of a new stealthy heavy bomber (the Pak DA) which will carry cruise missiles and, reportedly, hypersonic missiles.
- Development and deployment of the new Sarmat heavy ICBM with a mammoth 10 tons of throw-weight (which will, reportedly, carry 10 heavy or 15 medium nuclear warheads and hypersonic gliders) in 2018-2020.
- Development and deployment of the new Barguzin rail-mobile ICBM by 2018-2020.
- Development and deployment of a new "ICBM" called the RS-26 Rubezh, in reality, an intermediate-range missile, by 2016 or 2017.
- Development of a "fifth generation" missile submarine (the Husky) carrying ballistic and cruise missiles by 2020.
- Development of the new "Maritime Multifunctional System Status-6," a nuclear-armed, nuclear-powered, 10,000-km range, very fast, drone submarine capable of operating at a depth of 1,000-meters which the Russian press says carries a 100-megaton bomb and, possibly, a cobalt bomb.
- New improved versions of the SS-27 Mod 2/RS-24 and the Bulava-30 SLBM.

Senior Russian officials have stated that Russia is developing new types of nuclear weapons. In January 2005, then-Defense Minister Colonel General Sergei Ivanov declared, "We will develop, improve and deploy *new types* of nuclear weapons. We will make them more reliable and accurate"[130] (Emphasis added). In September 2009, Colonel General Vladimir Verkhovtsev, then-chief of the Defense Ministry's 12th Main Directorate, Russia's nuclear weapons organization, said the newly developed and manufactured nuclear munitions will have "improved tactical and technical specifications..."[131] The new and modernized delivery systems reportedly will carry everything from precision low yield and low collateral damage nuclear warheads to thermonuclear weapons with ultra-high yield.[132] The new Sarmat heavy ICBM apparently will become Russia's main counterforce weapon. There are at least three reports that Russia has deployed precision low yield nuclear weapons with yields between tens and 200 tons of TNT on their Bulava-30 and Sineva SLBMs.[133] The Russians have said that two of their new ICBMs will have conventional warhead options.[134] The new Russian nuclear-capable bombers are also being given much improved nuclear and conventional strike capability, including very long-range cruise missiles. They face no air defense capability of any significance from the U.S.

RUSSIAN TACTICAL NUCLEAR WEAPONS

In 2011, according to then-senior Obama administration NSC official Gary Samore, Russia had 10 times as many tactical nuclear weapons as the U.S (hundreds vs. thousands).[135] In 2012, the Obama administration estimated Russia had 4,000-6,500 nuclear weapons, 2,000-4,000 of which were tactical nuclear weapons.[136] In 2009, *TASS* said Russia probably had 15,000-17,000 nuclear weapons.[137]

The disparity is more than quantitative. Russian press reports indicate that Russian tactical nuclear forces include virtually every type of Cold War Soviet tactical nuclear weapon capability.[138] This includes short-range missiles, nuclear artillery, nuclear landmines, nuclear air and missile defense weapons, nuclear anti-ship missiles and bombs, nuclear depth charges, nuclear antisubmarine warfare missiles, nuclear torpedoes, nuclear bombs, coastal missile complexes, and the missiles of the Russian Air Force's and Navy's non-strategic aviation.[139]

Russian anti-access/area denial capability is being buttressed by systems that violate or circumvent the INF Treaty. In 2014, the Obama administration concluded Russia was violating the INF Treaty, calling this "a very serious matter."[140] It determined "that the Russian Federation was in violation of its obligations under the INF Treaty not to possess, produce, or flight-test a ground-launched cruise missile (GLCM) with a range capability of 500 km to 5,500 km, or to possess or produce launchers of such missiles."[141] This appears to be the tip of the iceberg. Russia seems to be negating the entire INF Treaty.

Russian battlefield nuclear weapons are particularly threatening to NATO Europe. Contrary to its arms control commitments, Russia has retained tactical nuclear missiles, artillery and atomic demolition munitions.[142] In April 2014, aAcademician Yevgeniy Avrorin, a former Director of the Sarov nuclear weapons laboratory (the All-Russian Scientific-Research Institute), in an interview published by the Sarov nuclear weapons laboratory, said the 152-mm nuclear artillery shell with "a kiloton yield" has been "broadly deployed" throughout the Russian Army.[143] In August 2016, Deputy NATO Secretary General Alexander Vershbow said the new Russian divisions are "backed by new air bases, naval forces and nuclear-capable short-range missiles."[144] During the Cold War, we had thousands of tactical nuclear weapons in Europe to deter the use of these types of weapons.[145] Except for the B-61 bomb, these are all gone.

RUSSIAN MISSILE AND AIR DEFENSES

Part of Russia's Soviet legacy was a massive air defense system and the world's only operational missile defenses. In modern Western terminology, these are "anti-access/area denial" weapons. According to General Frank Gorenc, the U.S. air advantage in Europe "is shrinking" and "the more alarming thing is their [Russia's] ability to create anti-access/area denied [zones] that are *very* well defended" by ground-based anti-aircraft missiles.[146] (Emphasis in the original). In 2016, General Robin Rand, Commander of Air Force Global Strike Command, told the House Armed Services Subcommittee on Strategic Forces that the Minuteman III will have a difficult time surviving in the active anti-access/area denial environment of the future and if it "is used to be a deterrent for this nation, then it needs to have a high probability that it will get to the target that it's intended for."[147] In the 1960s, Minuteman was reportedly provided chaff counter measures against the emerging Russian missile defenses,[148] obviously not the systems they now have or that they are about to deploy. For decades, there has been no indication of modern penetration devices on U.S. Minuteman and Trident missiles in Department of Defense presentations to the Congress.

Today, Russia is building what it calls an "aerospace defense" system designed to defend against all types of U.S. and NATO airborne and missile weapons. It has the potential to degrade both the U.S. nuclear deterrent and the ability of NATO to defend conventionally the weaker treaty members bordering Russia. In 2012, then-Lieutenant General Oleg Ostapenko, then- Aerospace Defense Troops commander, lists one of main functions of the Aerospace Defense forces as: "Destroying ICBM and SLBM warheads and destroying or functionally suppressing enemy military spacecraft."[149] In 2011, then-Russian Chief of the General Staff Nikolai Makarov announced that Russia's missile defenses would be "impenetrable."[150] They won't be, but they can erode our nuclear deterrent and our ability to use airpower to defend against a Russian conventional attack.

Russia will soon have two systems that can intercept ICBMs and SLBMs – the Moscow ABM system and the S-500. The Moscow ABM is being upgraded into the improved A-235 configuration.[151] Today, there are more ABM interceptors deployed at Moscow than the entire planned U.S. missile defense force. The main Russian defense against ICBMs and SLBMs will be the multirole S-500. Russian generals state that it is capable of intercepting ICBMs as well as medium-range missiles, airborne threats including aircraft, cruise missiles and hypersonic missiles and that the system is capable of intercepting missiles in near space.[152] Deputy Defense Minister Yuri Borisov said the S-500 "can destroy aerodynamic and ballistic targets of all types…"[153] Lieutenant General Ostapenko said that the S-500 can intercept "low-orbital satellites and space weapons" and "intercontinental ballistic missiles in the terminal phase of the trajectory and, within definite limits, in the midcourse sector."[154]

The S-500 will obviously be more capable than the new Russian S-400 against stealth aircraft and other types of air breathing targets. The announced S-500 range is 600-km, presumably against non-stealth aircraft.[155] Because of the limited range of many U.S. conventional air-launched cruise missiles, the S-500 has the potential to intercept many of the aircraft that carry them before the missiles can be launched. This could give Russia a significant advantage because U.S. land-based missile defenses, other than the Patriot, have no self-defense capability against aerodynamic threats. This is a direct result of designing systems against rogue state threats rather than against Russia.

In April 2015, Aerospace Forces Deputy Commander-in-Chief Lieutenant General Viktor Gumenny said that delivery of the S-500 system to the troops will begin "soon."[156] The announced Russian S-500 program involves the deployment of 10 battalions by 2020.[157] They will not likely make that date but their deployment is not likely to end at 10 battalions.

The new Russian S-400, with an announced intercept range of up to 400-km, is operational.[158] The Russians say the S-400 is capable of intercepting ballistic missiles with a velocity of 4.8-km per second (a range of about 3,000-km), bombers, and cruise missiles. The announced S-400 program involves the deployment of 56 battalions.[159]

The Russians are also deploying a new mobile SAM system called the S-300V4. They have just announced that it has a new 400-km range interceptor.[160] Former Almaz-Antey's Chief Designer Pavel Sozinov told *TASS* this "means that Airborne early warning and control aircraft, including AWACS (Airborne Warning and Control System), will now be unable to enter the 400-kilometer zone without repercussions."[161] Russia is also developing the medium-range mobile S-350E Vitaz.[162]

Russia's deployment of S-300 and S-400 systems to Syria and Iran significantly affected the threat equation in both states. Russia agreed to sell S-300s to Iran in 2007 but did not agree to deliver the missiles until an outline for the July 2015 nuclear agreement was announced in the spring of 2016. Iran claims the S-300s were delivered in August 2016 and will be used to defend its Fordow enrichment facility. Many experts believe these missiles were deployed at the Fordow facility to protect it from U.S. and Israeli airstrikes.

Russian officials announced in October 2016 that they had deployed S-300 missiles in Syria "to provide protection for the naval logistics facility in Tartus," Russia's naval base in Syria. However, IHS Jane's Defence Weekly said the deployment of these missiles to Syria was "a move apparently designed to deter US-led intervention in the Middle East country."[163] Fox News reported on October 4, 2016 that Russia deployed an S-400 missiles system to Syria after a Russian jet was shot down by a Turkish warplane last November.[164]

Russia has plans for missile defense beyond the S-500. In September 2011, Vladimir Kozin, a Deputy Director of the Russian Foreign Ministry's Information and Press Department, said that Russia was planning to develop its own sea-based missile defense system.[165] The former chief designer of Almaz-Antey Corporation, which develops Russia's air and missile defense systems, Igor Ashurbeili, has stated that the successor to the S-500 missile defense now under development will be air-based.[166]

Russia is in the process of improving its anti-access/area denial capabilities by the deployment of a number of types of advanced 4.5 generation fighters with improved intercept and strike capability. In 2018, Russia will begin to deploy what they call a 5th generation fighter, the Pak FA or Pak T-50.[167] In reality, it is apparently not a true 5th generation fighter but appears to outclass any of the Western 4.5 generation fighters.[168]

In 2013, four well-known Russian experts, Sergey Rogov, Colonel General (ret.) Viktor Yesin, Major General (ret.) Pavel Zolotarev and Vice-Admiral (ret.) Valentin Kuznetsov wrote that the "Global Zero" nuclear force of 450-900 weapons "clearly is insufficient for destroying all strategic targets on Russian territory," and, "If the Russian program for creating an aerospace defense is implemented, the number of targets to be destroyed in Russia will be reduced to approximately 10%."[169] In April 2015, Major General Kuril Makarov, Deputy Commander of Russia's Aerospace

Forces Command stated, "Moscow's layered air defense grants 99% effective defense against air attack..." due to deployment of S-400 and SA-20 defenses.[170]

Are we countering the capabilities of Russian advanced air and missile defenses? No, we are not. We are still 10-15 years away from any serious modernization of our deterrent forces and to date there is no announced program to enhance the ability of our strategic missiles to penetrate Russian or Chinese missile defenses.

RUSSIAN NUCLEAR HARDENING

In December 2015, Russia announced that it was reviving the Cold War program to provide the general population hardened shelters against nuclear attack.[171] In August 2016, Bill Gertz reported, "Russia is building large numbers of underground nuclear command bunkers in the latest sign Moscow is moving ahead with a major strategic forces modernization program. U.S. intelligence officials said construction has been underway for several years on 'dozens' of underground bunkers in Moscow and around the country."[172] Significantly, the Obama administration is now diminishing our ability to threaten very hard and deeply buried facilities by eliminating all of our high yield bombs.[173]

RUSSIAN ARMS CONTROL AND ARMS CONTROL NONCOMPLIANCE

Since the 1960s, arms control has played a largely negative role in enhancing U.S. national security. Except for the administrations of Ronald Reagan and George H.W. Bush, we have been out-negotiated by the Soviets and the Russians. The 1970s arms control negotiations failed to constrain the Soviet threat. Both the Soviet Union and Russia have ignored the legal constraints they accepted in these negotiations when it was in their interests. In December 1975, renowned British strategist Dr. Colin Gray, writing in *Air Force Magazine*, noted that the Soviets conducted arms control negotiations in "a fairly crudely combative way," and as part of a "political struggle."[174] In the words of former Under Secretary of Defense William Schneider, "A half-century of experience with successive administrations confronting Moscow's non-compliance suggests that the treaty-based approach to nuclear stability is fatally flawed."[175] The Reagan administration determined that the Soviets routinely violated arms control agreements. Its 1985 report to the Congress stated:

The Administration's most recent studies support its conclusion that there is a pattern of Soviet noncompliance. As documented in this and earlier reports, the Soviet Union has violated its legal commitments to the SALT I ABM Treaty and Interim Agreement, the SALT II agreement, the Limited Test Ban Treaty of 1963, the Biological and Toxin Weapons Convention, the Geneva Protocol on Chemical Weapons, and the Helsinki Final Act. In addition, the U.S.S.R. has likely violated provisions of the Threshold Test Ban Treaty.[176]

The Soviet legacy has shaped Russian views on arms control compliance.[177] In 2015, a House Armed Services Committee report noted:

According to the testimony of senior officials of the Department of State, the Russian Federation is not complying with numerous treaties and agreements, including the INF Treaty, the Open Skies Treaty, the Biological Weapons Convention, the Chemical Weapons Convention, the Vienna Document, the Budapest Memorandum, the Istanbul Commitments, the Presidential Nuclear Initiatives, the Missile Technology Control Regime, and the Russian Federation has recently withdrawn from the Treaty on Conventional Armed Forces in Europe (CFE).[178]

Since the conclusion of the New START Treaty in 2010, there have been no subsequent arms control negotiations with Russia.[179] In 2013, then-Kremlin Chief of Staff Sergei Ivanov explained why: "When I hear our American partners say: 'let's reduce something else', I would like to say to them: 'excuse me, but what we have is relatively new'. They [the U.S.] have not conducted any upgrades for a long time. They still use Trident [missiles]."[180] The end of arms control negotiations with Russia is a product of the failed "reset" policy and the weak negotiating approach of the State Department in New START. In New START, Russia got a treaty full of loopholes and a dramatically reduced verification regime, exactly what Russia wanted.[181]

In addition to the intermediate-range ground-launched cruise missile that the Obama administration has concluded is a violation of the INF Treaty, there are many other compliance issues being reported in the Russian press. In July 2010, Pavel Felgenhauer wrote "...Moscow plans to covertly quit the 1987 treaty on medium and short-range missiles" because the Russian S-300 and the S-400 air defense missiles, the new S-500 air and missile defense interceptor and the Moscow ABM interceptors are nuclear-armed and can function as "dual-use...conventional or nuclear medium- or shorter-range ballistic missiles."[182] If Felgenhauer is correct about these capabilities, at least two of the systems he mentioned (the Moscow ABM and the S-500) violate the INF Treaty.[183] If so, the whole nature of destruction of enemy air defense mission may have to be changed to include attacks against individual launchers. Another deployed Russian cruise missile, the R-500, reportedly has a range prohibited by the INF Treaty.[184]

Russia is reviving the INF-range ballistic missile threat to Europe and Asia through the deployment of the RS-26 Rubezh, an IRBM masquerading as an ICBM.[185] According to state-run *Sputnik News* it carries four 300-kt warheads.[186] This missile is potentially a violation of the INF and the New START Treaties.[187] Indeed, it may not be able to fly to ICBM range with its normal payload.[188] According to *Rossiyskaya Gazeta*, a Russian Government daily newspaper, it has "a combat radius from 2,000 km."[189]

Thanks to U.S. compliance with the INF Treaty and other commitments made in the 1991-1992 Presidential Nuclear Initiatives, there are no U.S. conventional or nuclear theater missiles or battlefield nuclear weapons in NATO Europe and Asia.[190] In 2004, Assistant Secretary of State Stephen Rademaker voiced Washington's concern that Russia "has not fully met its commitments [under the Presidential Nuclear Initiatives or PNIs of 1991-1992] to reduce tactical nuclear weapons in Europe."[191] Russia has violated its pledges with regard to elimination of some types of tactical nuclear weapons including battlefield nuclear weapons.[192] Hence, Russia has an unprecedented advantage in systems that could be used against a NATO counter attack if Russia, for example, invades the weak Baltic NATO states.

There has been a fundamental disconnect between U.S. nuclear weapons arms control policy and U.S. national interests. Since the end of the Cold War, we have not modernized our strategic forces with new systems and we have also reduced their numbers. Yet historically, we have depended upon numbers to negate Soviet and now Russian missile defenses. In the 1960s, we deployed chaff packages on Minuteman ICBMs against the emerging Soviet missile defenses.[193] Since the late 1960s Poseidon SLBM, we have depended upon large numbers of warheads to deal with defenses. There is no indication in Congressional testimony going back many decades of the placement of penetration devices on our Trident missiles. Thus, we have been making Russian missile defenses more effective while deploying a missile defense system that has virtually no capability against Russian ballistic missiles.[194]

CHART 1

New START Treaty Shrinks U.S. Arsenal, Permits Russian Growth

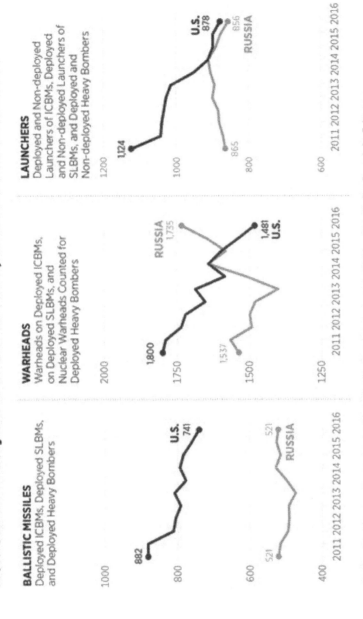

BALLISTIC MISSILES
Deployed ICBMs, Deployed SLBMs, and Deployed Heavy Bombers

WARHEADS
Warheads on Deployed ICBMs, on Deployed SLBMs, and Nuclear Warheads Counted for Deployed Heavy Bombers

LAUNCHERS
Deployed and Non-deployed Launchers of ICBMs, Deployed and Non-deployed Launchers of SLBMs, and Deployed and Non-deployed Heavy Bombers

NOTE: Biannual figures for each year are for March and September, except for 2011 in which the first figure is for February.
SOURCE: U.S. Department of State, Bureau of Verification, Compliance, and Implementation, "New START: Fact Sheets,"
http://www.state.gov/t/avc/newstart/c39906.htm (accessed May 23, 2016).

BG 3078 ⚫ heritage.org

50

The following chart by Michaela Dodge of the Heritage Foundation plot Russian and U.S. declared numbers since the New START Treaty's entry-into-force.[195] They indicate that the reductions in strategic forces have almost entirely been made by the U.S. and deployed Russian warheads have significantly increased in numbers. Thus far, former Duma Defense Committee Vice Chairman Aleksey Arbatov has been correct when he said in 2010 that New START was "essentially a treaty on limiting the American strategic forces."[196]

As the 2016 National Institute for Public Policy report on Russian strategy concluded, "Russian threats, including nuclear threats, its robust nuclear force modernization program, and its pattern of violating arms control agreements—particularly the 1987 Intermediate Nuclear Forces (INF) Treaty—appear to be integral elements in the broad Russian grand strategy..."[197] Russia, which is expanding its nuclear forces, uses arms control to facilitate its nuclear strategy by avoiding effective limitations and cheating when necessary. It was foolish to degrade the legacy START Treaty verification regime in New START and to create loopholes that can be used to expand forces beyond the notional limitations in New START. According to *Russia Today*, General Nikolai Makarov, Chief of the Russian General Staff, stated, *"The new START is the first treaty that satisfies us."*[198] *(Emphasis in the original.)* The Senate Foreign Relations Committee's Republican minority report accurately pointed out, "New START is a bad deal coming and going: it neither places effective limits on a future Russian renewal of its strategic nuclear forces (the beginnings of which already can be seen), nor does it demand real Russian reductions now. This the Obama administration touts as a great negotiating accomplishment."[199]

In October 2016, *TASS* reported, "Russian President Vladimir Putin has ordered suspension of the plutonium disposal agreement (the 2000 Plutonium Disposition and Management Agreement) with the United States over Washington's unfriendly actions towards Russia."[200] "Suspend" is Russian political spin meaning "withdraw" from the agreement which mandated that 34 tons of plutonium be transferred from the Russian nuclear weapons program to peaceful uses.[201] This appears to be an implementation of a standard Russian nuclear related threat of terminating arms control agreements. We may see the same type of threat next year related to the New START Treaty.

CONCLUSION

Putin's Russia is preparing for war against the U.S. and NATO. Putin would prefer to win without fighting, but he is prepared to use force and apparently escalate to nuclear weapons use if it is necessary and in Russia's interests. He must be deterred. We are not doing nearly enough to do so. Current policy runs a risk of deterrent failure and further Russian and Chinese military aggression. To deter Russia we must be able prevail quickly in high intensity conflict and deter nuclear first use. High minded speeches about nuclear zero will not accomplish these objectives.

Russia's New Military in the Service of Old Ambitions

By Daniel Gouré

As events in Crimea, Eastern Ukraine and Syria have unfolded, the world has had a chance to see the new Russian military strategy and many elements of its force posture in action. Russian President Putin has successfully finessed his country's myriad of weaknesses – economic, political, demographic and military – in ways that permit him to use coercion and even naked military force against his neighbors with near impunity. Dealing with an aggressive, yet relatively weak Russia poses a far different problem for the West than deterring or containing a rising China.

Moreover, the kind of military Russia is developing may be particularly well suited to the Kremlin's objective of undermining the existing international security order and gaining recognition of Russian great power status with a limited risk of war. The "new" Russian military has a demonstrated a particular mix of capabilities – rapid, but geographically limited offensive operations, electronic and cyber warfare, long-range precision strikes, powerful anti-access/area denial systems and advanced theater and strategic nuclear weapons– that well serve the goals of supporting gray area operations and deterring Western conventional responses or escalatory moves.

The discussions of Russian "hybrid" warfare should not obscure an understanding of the extent to which that country has modernized its conventional and nuclear forces and the extent to which it is relying not on gray zone techniques but conventional military forces as the centerpiece of its local aggressions. It is important also to recognize how much Russian adventures in Eastern Europe have rapidly morphed from hybrid operations employing non-traditional means and methods to classic conventional military operations. The recent intervention in Syria was a model power projection operation suggesting that the Russian military was quite capable of limited high intensity conventional operations. According to Chatham House Senior Fellow Dr. Andrew Monaghan:

> Indeed, the hybrid label serves to draw a veil over the conventional aspects of the war in Eastern Ukraine. While non-military means of power were deployed, they relied on more traditional conventional measures for their success. This was

amply demonstrated in the battles at Debaltsevo, Donbass airport and Ilovaisk, during which much of the fighting involved high intensity combat, including the extensive use of armor, artillery and multiple launch rocket systems, as well as drones and electronic warfare. During these battles, massed bombardments were deployed to considerable lethal effect – in short but intense bombardments battalion sized units were rendered inoperable, suffering heavy casualties.[202]

A NEW CONVENTIONAL FORCE STRUCTURE WITH A TRADITIONAL OPERATIONAL CONCEPT

The most significant aspects of the Russian military's modernization effort have to do not with new and more capable weapons systems but with structural reforms, most notably the reduction in the overall size of the military and the number of units, the increased focus on professionalizing all levels of service and the creation of a relatively small set of well-trained, manned and equipped land, sea and air forces. The result of these efforts, albeit not yet completed, has been to provide the Kremlin with a force designed for rapid, high intensity conventional operations within a geographically limited zone that corresponds largely to the boundaries of the former Soviet Union/Warsaw Pact.

The new Russian theater force structure has four essential components. First, a limited number of highly capable, rapidly deployable and very mobile formations, a combination of Special Forces (Spetznaz), airborne and light infantry brigades, manned disproportionately by professional soldiers. These provide both an offensive element and a rapid response defensive capability. Second, a conventional Army consisting of an increasingly standardized set of armored, motorized infantry and artillery/missile brigades that are slowly being equipped with modernized tanks, APCs, artillery and missile systems. Increasingly the artillery and rocket forces are the key offensive force element, being organized and equipped to execute a paralyzing first strike on opposing theater forces. Third, an expanding, increasingly sophisticated air defense capability resident in both the Army and Air Force. This capability is not only designed for the defense of Russian territory but also to deny access to critical airspace over foreign countries, particularly NATO's eastern members. Finally, a supporting Air Force and naval strike capability, elements of which were clearly demonstrated during the Syrian intervention. New command and control structures and support capabilities (e.g., logistics, ISR and medical) are being put in place to enable these forces to operate more jointly, rapidly and at greater distances from the Russian border.[203]

The strategic implications of this capability for Moscow were described by General Phillip Breedlove, former NATO SACEUR, thusly

> They are absolutely able to bring great force to a position of readiness. That is something that we have to think about: What does that mean geo-strategically that we now have a nation that can produce this ready force and now has demonstrated that it will use that ready force to go across a sovereign boundary?[204]

As the eminent expert on Russian political and military issues, Dr. Stephen Blank, points out, current Russian operational thinking has long-standing antecedents. In classic Soviet fashion, the modern Russian General Staff has been planning for the kinds of operations observed in recent years, organizing the necessary forces and defining the kinds of technical capabilities needed to implement the desired strategy. According to Blank,

> The war against Ukraine is not a "new" strategy for Moscow; the Russian general staff has been preparing for Ukraine-type combat operations since 1999. Indeed, the Ukrainian operation has been planned by Moscow at least since 2005 . . .
>
> The Russian military's Zapad 2013 exercise (the word 'Zapad' meaning 'West' in Russian to denote that it was an operation designed to practice operations against NATO) was a dress-rehearsal for parts of the Ukraine campaign and future potential operations against the Baltic states.[205]

Moscow also is engaged in a program to create a ring of bases designed to counter what the Kremlin asserts is a Western policy of encircling Russia. New air and ground force bases have been established in western Russia and Belarus. Putin's regime is establishing a string of facilities in the Arctic including in space that are considered international waters. Russian sources have floated the idea of a return of military forces to Cuba and Vietnam. Most recently, Russia announced that it was expanding its bases in Syria into permanent naval and air facilities and deploying advanced air defense systems that reach far into neighboring countries. These activities not only provide an outer defense ring for the homeland but create the basis for threatening horizontal escalation in the event of a confrontation with the U.S. or NATO.[206]

While much has been made of the Russian use of so-called asymmetric tools and techniques in the operations against Crimea and Ukraine, the reality is that is relatively little in the Russian strategy for political-military warfare that is truly new. It is true that the Kremlin is forging ahead on its military modernization program intended to replace some 70% of Soviet-era equipment by 2020. Force structure is being revamped, command and control streamlined and weapons systems improved. It also has trained certain elements of its conventional force structure to support unconventional or so-called hybrid operations. But in many ways, what has been seen over the past few years suggests an arc of development in the future that in many ways reflect the Soviet-era roots of the current Russian government and military. A recent NATO analysis explains the continuities between the current Putinist approach to its Soviet-era political and military warfare concepts concludes this way:

> In sum, it could be argued that Moscow's non-linear warfare understanding reflects a "new" or "renewed" Russian military thought, not a strategy or concept. It is renewed thinking as it combines the Soviet-legacy Deep Operations Theory and Reflexive Control Theory in order to create a "disguised blitzkrieg impact." In doing so, Moscow uses a core group of elite troops along with a wide array of non-military means while concealing its true geopolitical intentions and surreptitiously influencing its competitors' decision-making algorithms.[207]

NEW RUSSIAN CONVENTIONAL CAPABILITIES

There is no question that the military modernization program begun in the mid-2000s has been more successful than many observers at the time expected. The Russian Ministry of Defense simplified the overall command structure, reduced the number of units to a manageable set of fully staffed and equipped formations and developed an exercise and training regime to support rapid concentration and deployment.

A focused modernization program has now provided the military, but especially the ground forces, with a set of new capabilities focused, in particular, on countering well-documented U.S. and NATO advantages. What some sources have described as Russian "New Generation" warfare includes, in addition to information operations, new operational concepts, innovative tactics and weapons systems:

- Electronic warfare
- Unmanned aerial systems
- Massed fires with advanced warheads and sub-munitions
- Combined arms brigades with new armored vehicles
- Air assault and Special Operations brigades
- Advanced, mobile anti-aircraft systems, and
- Combined kinetic and cyber strike operations.[208]

The Russian government has matched its reforms in military organization with an impressive, albeit unfinished, program to modernize the technological base of its armed forces. The state armaments program for 2011-2020 seeks to increase the total percentage of modern weaponry in the Russian armed forces from approximately 10% in 2008 to around 70% in 2020. The program set very precise goals for weapons acquisitions including addition of 600 aircraft and 1,100 helicopters for the air force. This will include at least ten T-50 fifth generation stealth aircraft. The navy is scheduled to receive no fewer than 100 ships, including 25 corvettes, 14-15 frigates and 24 submarines. The last includes 8 Borey-class SSBNs (ballistic missile submarines) armed with the new R-30 Bulava type SLBM (submarine-launched ballistic missile). The army is scheduled to receive 2,300 tanks, 2,000 artillery pieces, 400 S-400 and 100 S-500 air and missile defense systems and 120 Iskander-M short range ballistic missile launchers for the army. The success of this program is critically dependent on levels of defense spending and on the ability of the defense industries to deal with both quality control and critical parts problems. [209]

Another of the successes of the Russian military modernization program is its Special Operations Forces (SOF). Following the near-debacle of the 2008 war with Georgia, the Russian government revamped its Special Operations command and control structure and focused on increasing the capabilities of SOF units. It paid particular attention to enhancing the ability of these forces to conduct counter-terrorism and subversion operations. In addition, the Russian military focused on combining deployments of Special Operations Forces on the ground with new tactics and techniques for counter-C3 (command, control and communications) warfare, including expanded cyber attacks.

Perhaps the most striking aspect of this modernization effort is the improvements provided to the Russian army. As numerous observers and analysts have remarked, Russian operations in Ukraine demonstrate not only significant enhancements in operational and tactical actions but a range of improved technologies and their integration into a true combined arms capability. According to Rand Corporation senior researcher Dr. David Johnson,

> Russian and separatist forces are employing combined arms warfare with advanced weapons to devastating effect. Russian artillery, particularly rocket launchers with conventional, thermobaric, and cluster munitions—using unmanned aerial systems (UAS), both for target location and battle damage assessment – is particularly effective against Ukrainian light armor and infantry formations. Additionally, the Russians are using their most advanced tanks in the Ukraine, including the T-72B3, T-80, and T-90. All of these tanks have 125mm guns capable of firing a wide range of ammunition, including antitank/anti-helicopter missiles with a six-kilometer range, and advanced armor

protection, including active protection on some models. Finally, the Russian air defense systems (man-portable and vehicle mounted) have made it all but suicidal for the Ukrainian Air Force to provide air support to ground forces. Thus, the battlefields of Eastern Ukraine are similar to those envisioned by the U.S. Army during the Cold War, but with more mature technologies.[210]

In a number of cases, the improvements demonstrated by the Russian Army are not simply improvements on existing capabilities, although that too is in the works, but truly revolutionary capabilities. Colonel (ret.) James B. Hickey explained in an August 2016 statement:

> Last May, Russia paraded its Armata Universal Combat Platform in Red Square. Russia designed, tested, and produced this vehicle in six years. Albeit still in development, this design is a basis for a family of combat vehicles that is intended to be the back bone of highly mobile, combined arms force capable of great hitting power. The Armata tank and infantry carrier variants will exploit a revolutionary design with improved target detection, fire control, mobility; range, and both active and reactive armor protection. Additionally, Russia is well on its way to modernizing and standardizing legacy armored vehicle designs to make them effective on the 21st century combined arms battlefield.[211]

By all estimates, the advances shown in Russian electronic warfare (EW) have been nothing short of remarkable. Russian EW units have demonstrated the ability to "black out" opposing military and even national communications.[212] Lieutenant General Ben Hodges, the Commander, US Army in Europe remarked in a 2015 interview that:

> The Russians have continued to move forward with their EW modernization. They have demonstrated the ability to completely shut down everything the Ukrainians are using in terms of communications. OSCE has reported that the drones they use for monitoring are being interfered with. Again, this is not something you can craft in your basement. There is imagery, public pictures of Russian systems in Crimea that are absolute state of the art.[213]

Advances in Russian artillery and missiles, the latter not limited to the ground forces, presents not only a tactical challenge to NATO and the U.S. but a significant operational threat as well. The combination of unmanned aerial vehicles and concentrated artillery fire using advanced precision munitions has proven particularly effective in the Ukraine.[214]

What is particularly noteworthy is that the Russian military has demonstrated an ability to integrate different systems as well as force elements. The Russian Army has developed a fairly sophisticated indirect fires capability that employs electronic warfare, unmanned aerial systems for intelligence, surveillance and reconnaissance

(ISR) and targeting and the rapid delivery of massed artillery and rocket fires. Electronic warfare is applied across the conflict spectrum and integrated with information operations, cyber attacks and the actions of Special Operations units. Bret Perry, an analyst with Avascent, wrote in a 2016 article:

> Moscow has proven adept at using EW and SOF *[Special Operations Forces]* in concert to fragment and slow adversaries' strategic decision-making. While "little green men" secure key locations and train local forces, electronic-warfare forces distort ISR collection by adversaries and third parties, limiting their ability to project an accurate counter-narrative to inform confused domestic audiences and a divided international community. And even when a defender does manage to grasp the situation, Russian EW attacks on their command, control, communications, and intelligence disrupts their response.[215]

In addition, the Russian military has been working diligently to improve their long-range conventional and dual-capable strike systems. From launch positions in Kaliningrad and the Western Military District, the Iskander M can cover the Baltics, most of Poland and portions of Germany, Denmark and Sweden. The 2,500 km range of the Kalibr'/Klub systems will enable them to cover virtually all of Western Europe from sites in Western Russia.[216]

During the recent operation in Syria, the Russian military sought to send the world a multi-level message with its strikes on targets in that country with cruise missiles fired from the Caspian Sea. According to Stephen Blank,

> The firing of the Kalibr' cruise missile from a frigate in the Caspian Sea 900 KM away from Syria to mark Putin's birthday on October 7, 2015 is not only an homage to the president but demonstrates the potential for combining power projection with long-range strikes from "privileged sanctuaries" inside Russia. And of course it also highlights potential new missions for Russia's navy in tandem with air and/or ground forces.[217]

Operations by Russian forces in Eastern Europe will take place beneath a very capable and growing anti-access/area denial (A2/AD) umbrella. The commander of U.S. Air Forces in Europe, General Frank Gorenc, warned that the surface-to-air missile systems now deployed in Kaliningrad are "layered in a way that makes access to that area difficult." Longer-range Russian systems are capable of threatening NATO aircraft operating in parts of Poland and the Baltics.[218] Crimea is now being turned into another A2/AD bastion that will not only protect Russia's southern flank but essentially grant it control over the Black Sea. The intervention in Syria has enabled Moscow to create an air defense bubble not only over parts of that country but well into the Eastern Mediterranean. Former Supreme Allied Commander

Europe, retired U.S. Air Force General Philip Breedlove, described the Russian A2/AD problem this way:

> We have the tools, but we do not have nearly enough of them – and the speed that we would need to eliminate these A2/AD bubbles – to be able to deploy our forces is going to be controlled by the depth of the bench of how we can attack those A2/AD forces. . . Right now, we're almost completely dependent on air forces and aviation assets in order to attack the A2/AD problem . . . We need more long-range, survivable, precision strike capability from the ground . . .We need dense capability – like the dense A2/AD networks that we face. [219]

Over the past three years, the Russian armed forces have conducted no fewer than18 large-scale exercises, some of which have involved more than 100,000 troops and several of which simulated nuclear attacks against NATO allies.[220] The Zapad 2013 exercise, which took place in the Baltic region involved the deployment of an estimated 70,000 troops including land, sea, air, air defense, airborne, Special Forces, Internal Troops of the Ministry of Interior, medical units and army psychological personnel, logistical and engineering forces. Among the missions demonstrated were: search and rescue; amphibious landing and anti-landing; air and ground strikes on enemy targets; submarine and anti-submarine warfare; missile strikes with long-range precision strike assets; and airborne and air assault operations.[221]

The current Russian military buildup is driven by a strategic vision of full spectrum dominance involving capabilities to conduct rapid decisive operations in space, cyber space, air, land and naval domains. In the view of Stephen Blank,

> To judge from its procurements, the current large-scale comprehensive buildup of weaponry through 2025 aims to acquire a multi-domain, strategic-level reconnaissance-strike complex as well as a tactical-level reconnaissance-fire complex that would together give Russia high-tech precision forces that could conduct operations in space, under the ocean, in the air, on the sea and the ground, and in cyberspace. This force would have parity with the U.S. and NATO in conventional and nuclear dimensions of high-tech warfare, and therefore the capability to deter and intimidate NATO. It would also have strategic stability, which Russia defines to include non-nuclear strike capabilities, and therefore sustain non-nuclear and pre-nuclear (i.e., before conflict starts) conventional deterrence across the entire spectrum of conflict, including against internal threats, which now feature prominently in Russia's defense doctrine.[222]

EVOLVING NUCLEAR CAPABILITIES AND CONCEPTS

The final area where Russian defense investments have paid off is in nuclear weapons. Russia is a major power because it, along with the United States, is the largest nuclear weapons state in the world. With respect to theater nuclear weapons, the Russian inventory is estimated to be ten times that of the United States. Russia is modernizing every part of its nuclear force posture. In May 2016, Russia announced the deployment of a massive new intercontinental ballistic missile (ICBM), a replacement for the aging SS-18. This missile, the RS-28 Sarmat – dubbed by the Western media 'Son of Satan" or the 'Satan II' – will be the world's largest nuclear missile and due to be operational in 2016. The RS-28 reportedly can reportedly carry a payload between 4 to 10 tons. At 10 tons, it will be able to carry 10 heavy or 15 medium independently-targeted thermonuclear warheads.[223]

Russia is modernizing the rest of its ICBM force, deploying an advanced submarine that will carry a new ballistic missile and adding dual capable cruise and ballistic missiles to its theater land and sea forces.

It is clear that Russia has violated the 1987 INF Treaty by developing cruise and ballistic missiles that exceed permissible ranges. The 2014, 2015 and 2015 State Department reports *Adherence to and Compliance with Arms Control, Nonproliferation, and Disarmament Agreements and Commitments* have all stated that Moscow is in violation of its INF Treaty obligations. The 2016 report declared that:

> the cruise missile developed by Russia meets the INF Treaty definition of a ground-launched cruise missile with a range capability of 500 km to 5,500 km, and as such, all missiles of that type, and all launchers of the type used or tested to launch such a missile, are prohibited under the provisions of the INF Treaty.[224]

Nuclear weapons are at the heart of Putin's geo-political strategy for reasserting Russian influence not only in the near-abroad but also in Europe as a whole. The Kremlin believes that if Europe remains vulnerable to Russian nuclear threats it can be influenced, even coerced on subjects such as Ukraine. In effect, Moscow hopes that this threat will encourage NATO and the EU to stand by as the Russian empire is recreated. According to the former head of the Russian General Staff, Yuri Baluyevsky: the purpose of expanding the inventory of short-range, nuclear armed ballistic missiles was "to erect a system of national security assurance" with missiles that could target cities in Poland, Romania, and the Baltic and, as a result, "cool the heads of these states leaders."[225] Nuclear weapons also play a crucial role in deterring threats from NATO and the United States until such time, estimated to be 2025 in Russian strategic assessments, advances in modern weaponry will permit Moscow to create a regime of conventional deterrence.

It is with these objectives in mind that Russia has been developing a series of launchers and warheads to permit it to conduct precision low yield nuclear strikes. These weapons are consistent with the Russian military doctrine's focus on being able to employ a limited number of relatively low yield weapons so as to counter Western conventional superiority and de-escalate a conflict with NATO. Recent major Russian exercises in the Western Military District have focused in part on the use of tactical and theater nuclear weapons for the purpose of controlling escalation.[226]

One of the primary reasons that Russia has been so steadfastly opposed to the deployment of missile defenses in Europe, even though proposed defenses will be incapable of defeating Russian strategic nuclear forces, is because it is concerned that such capabilities will devalue their nuclear weapons as instruments of coercion with respect to Europe. For this reason, the hint put forward recently by the Obama Administration that it is considering accelerating the deployment of theater missile defenses, the Phased Adaptive Approach, to Eastern Europe, is a significant threat to the Kremlin.

The Kremlin has become extremely adept at using the threat of nuclear conflict to intimidate NATO. For a number of years, Russian leaders have warned that they might use theater nuclear weapons against missile defense sites in Romania and Poland. In October, the Kremlin announced that it was moving its advanced, dual-capable, mobile Iskander theater ballistic missile into the Kaliningrad enclave. From there, the missies can even hold Berlin at risk.[227]

CONCLUSION

The successful occupation of Crimea and the current operations to destabilize Eastern Ukraine belie the general weakness of Russia's conventional military forces. Successive modernization campaigns have run afoul of budget difficulties, weaknesses in the country's military-industrial complex, the inability to shift from a conscript-based to a professional military, a limited pool of acceptable conscripts and political infighting. Efforts to mimic Western militaries' transformation from quantity to quality in military forces have been only partly successful. Despite a significant increase in defense spending in recent years, the Russian military not only lacks sufficient modern equipment, but also lacks many of the critical enablers to support the kind of high intensity, fast-paced, information-intensive operations that the United States and a number of its allies can conduct. Russia has had to go to foreign suppliers, including NATO countries, for such capabilities as amphibious warfare ships, unmanned aerial vehicles and even training facilities.

Nonetheless, Russia has developed and demonstrated a capability for conducting a kind of quasi-military campaign designed to achieve ends equivalent to those formerly attainable only by military means but with a diminished risk of actual war with NATO. According to a report by the Defense Committee of the UK Parliament:

> The Russian deployment of asymmetric tactics represents a new challenge to NATO. Events in Ukraine demonstrate in particular Russia's ability to effectively paralyze an opponent in the pursuit of its interests with a range of tools including psychological operations, information warfare and intimidation with massing of conventional forces. Such operations may be designed to slip below NATO's threshold for reaction. In many circumstances, such operations are also deniable, increasing the difficulties for an adversary in mounting a credible and legitimate response.[228]

Many Western leaders and defense analysts focus too much on the actual capabilities of the Russian military to engage in a high-end conventional conflict. The Russian military is an extremely brittle instrument. It will be decades, if ever, before Russia will pose a conventional threat to NATO writ large. Rather, it is the role of Russian conventional capabilities as an escalatory threat and a backstop to its quasi-military activities that is most threatening. According to Chatham House fellow Keir Giles,

> In any case, Russia does not need to mount an actual invasion in order to use military intimidation against its neighbors. The Crimea operation demonstrated that it is already willing to use those parts of its military it considers fit for purpose, while the main force is still being developed. In the meantime, Russia's Ground Troops created effect simply by existing. Throughout much of 2014 and early 2015, the main force opposite the Ukrainian border served as a distraction from actual operations within Ukraine, by being depleted or augmented as the political situation dictated, keeping Western governments and intelligence agencies in a perpetual state of speculation as to the likelihood of a full-scale invasion. The actual capability of those troops was irrelevant; they were ready and available to be inserted into Ukraine as and when required to counter Ukrainian government offensives.[229]

In addition, Moscow may believe that its superiority in theater nuclear weapons and a modernized strategic nuclear force posture allows it the option of escalation in response to a failed or stalled asymmetric/conventional offensive. The

Russian reliance on nuclear forces both for deterrence and escalation control is likely to increase over time, despite the desire to create a conventional deterrent based on advanced weapons and a new force structure. One of the primary reasons for this is Russia's demographic disaster which makes even filling the ranks of the current, smaller force. Another reason is Russia's long-term budgetary challenges. Nuclear weapons are cheaper than an effective advanced conventional deterrent and in the case of Russia, much easier to build and maintain.

The Kremlin knows it has neither the time nor the resources to reconstruct a great power military. It must act in the near term to create the conditions that will, in effect, insulate Russia from the forces of global economic and political change. The West will have to figure out how to help those living in Russia's neighborhood withstand the kind of tactics and forces Moscow employed in Crimea and is currently employing in Eastern Ukraine, pose a credible counter to Russian conventional forces and deter the threats posed by that country's long-range conventional and nuclear weapons.

Russian Economic Warfare

By Kevin Freeman

Few people make the connection that the struggle between the old USSR and the United States was as much an economic war as anything else. President Reagan understood this and appropriately used economic means to defeat the Soviet Union and force the tear down of the Berlin Wall.[230] His awareness and corresponding action forever altered the history of the world.

The idea of an economic war, however, was not lost on the Soviets. In fact, they understood better than so many in the West that the battle between communism and capitalism was indeed all about economics. Even at the height of military tensions, the final Soviet victory plan was always based in economics. Vladimir Putin would have been well acquainted with this perspective based on his time at the KGB, and carried forward the plans when he first assumed the Russian Presidency.

In September 1998, as Putin was plotting his 2000 rise as national leader, a Russian professor named Igor Panarin made a bold prediction regarding the United States while speaking at a conference in Linz, Austria. Panarin shocked the 400 delegates when he explained his theory that the United States was destined to collapse, dissolving into six separate blocs.[231] At the time, his thoughts seemed preposterous. If it weren't for the fact that Panarin had a background as a KGB analyst and was dean of the Russian Foreign Ministry's academy for future diplomats, he might have been laughed out of the room.[232] After all, the United States was dominating the world militarily, economically, and in virtually every respect. It was Russia that was in trouble, at the beginning of a massive currency crisis and on the heels of a 75% drop in its stock market. Russia defaulted on its debt and its very continuation as a sovereign nation was called into question. Yet, at that very moment in world history, a Russian professor with a KGB background was predicting the demise of the United States and the emergence of Russia and China leading the world in less than two decades.

It is perhaps important to note that Igor Panarin was, and remains, a friend of Vladimir Putin and a strident political supporter.[233] What he shared in Austria in 1998 was no doubt more than an intellectual observation. Exactly 10 years later, the

United States entered its own financial crisis with the collapse of Lehman Brothers that seemingly paralleled Panarin's prediction and echoed the serious problems of Russia a decade earlier. Panarin boldly proclaimed the demise of the United States would be caused by a financial collapse, calling our debt a "pyramid scheme." Interestingly, America's foreign debt was actually declining when Panarin first made the prediction. In the late 1990s, our economy was on such a strong path that the White House's Office of Management and Budget forecast that we would pay off all Federal debt by the year 2010. In hindsight, it appears clear that Panarin may have known something that the White House did not.

We believe that Panarin understood that the nature of war was changing and that the traditional American military approach was ill-equipped for newer forms of warfare to emerge in the 21st century. Less than six months after Panarin's prediction, two senior Chinese Army colonels wrote a seminal book explaining the war of the future titled *Unrestricted Warfare* in which they wrote:

> Thus, financial war is a form of non-military warfare which is just as terribly destructive as a bloody war, but in which no blood is actually shed. Financial warfare has now officially come to war's center stage – a stage that for thousands of years has been occupied only by soldiers and weapons, with blood and death everywhere. We believe that before long, 'financial warfare' will undoubtedly be an entry in the various types of dictionaries of official military jargon. Moreover, when people revise the history books on twentieth-century warfare in the early 21st century, the section on financial warfare will command the reader's utmost attention.[234]

Panarin, like the Chinese, viewed the 1998 Russian crisis as a casualty of a U.S.-led global economy and to a certain extent a victim of financial warfare.[235] What he projected for the United States in 2010 may have been more than simple observation or even wishful thinking. In fact, it is eerily reminiscent of KGB strategy articulated by Jan Sejna, one of the highest-ranking Soviet–bloc defectors in history. Sejna, in his 1982 book, *We Will Bury You*, explained the plan (emphasis added):

> "By fostering belief in our policy of friendship and co-operation with America, we planned to receive the greatest possible economic and technological help from the West, and at the same time convince the capitalist countries that they had no need of military alliances . . . The fourth and final phase of the Plan looked forward to the dawn of 'Global Democratic Peace.' At the start of Phase Four the U.S. would be isolated from both Europe and the developing countries. We could therefore undermine it by the use of external economic weapons, and so create the social and economic conditions for progressive forces to emerge inside the country."

What would constitute an external economic weapon? When put into context with an understanding of the Russian currency crisis of 2008 and the Chinese concept of financial warfare, it becomes obvious that one such weapon could include the targeting another nation's stock market, sovereign debt, and currency. Now, consider these comments from Vladimir Putin about the United States:

> They are living beyond their means and shifting a part of the weight of their problems to the world economy . . . They are living like parasites off the global economy and their monopoly of the dollar.

According to a 2013 Bloomberg report, Putin not only railed against the dollar, but also has been actively betting against it, "putting his money where his mouth is," so to speak.[236]

In 2008, based on comments from former Treasury Secretary Hank Paulson, Russia went further than simply betting against our economy. Putin appears to have concocted a scheme to directly attack. According to a January 2010 Bloomberg story:

> The Russians made a 'top-level approach' to the Chinese 'that together they might sell big chunks of their GSE holdings to force the U.S. to use its emergency authorities to prop up these companies,' Paulson said, referring to the acronym for government sponsored entities. The Chinese declined, he said."

> 'The report was deeply troubling – heavy selling could create a sudden loss of confidence in the GSEs and shake the capital markets,' Paulson wrote. 'I waited till I was back home and in a secure environment to inform the president.'"

> Russia sold all of its Fannie and Freddie debt in 2008, after holding $65.6 billion of the notes at the start of that year, according to central bank data. Fannie and Freddie were seized by regulators on Sept. 6, 2008, amid the worst U.S. housing slump since the Great Depression.

> Paulson said he was surprised not to have been asked about the Fannie and Freddie bonds during a trip to Moscow in June. "I was soon to learn, though, that the Russians had been doing a lot of thinking about our GSE securities," he said of his meeting with Dmitry Medvedev, who succeeded Putin in the Kremlin the previous month.[237]

Even though the Russians denied scheming to dump bonds in 2008, four things are very clear. First, they did dump their Fannie and Freddie bonds as the record clearly shows. Second, this action did undermine our economy at a critical juncture. The systematic dumping of over $65 billion of Fannie Mae and Freddie Mac bonds during the summer of 2008 magnified and extended the crisis with continuing effects today.

Third, it should be understood that the foreign dumping of bonds is considered to be deployment of a powerful economic weapon. This is made clear in a 2011 article in the Qiushi Journal, the official publication of the Communist Party of China. In February 2011, the *Times of India* published these excerpts from this article in English:

> Of course, to fight the US, we have to come up with key weapons. What is the most powerful weapon China has today? It is our economic power, especially our foreign exchange reserves (USD 2.8 trillion). The key is to use it well. If we use it well, it is a weapon...
>
> China must have enough courage to challenge the US currency. China can act in one of two ways. One is to sell US dollar reserves, and the second is not to buy US dollars for a certain period of time, which will weaken the currency and cause deep economic crisis for Washington...
>
> If China stops buying, other countries will pay close attention and are very likely to follow.
>
> Once the printed excess dollars cannot be sold, the depreciation of the dollar will accelerate and the impact on Americans wealth will be enormous..." This approach, it said, is market-driven and it will not be able to easily blame China. The US will not be able to withstand this pressure.[238]

Thus, when the Chinese told Secretary Paulson that the Russians asked them to join in dumping our bonds, they understood this suggestion to mean that the nations together would use external economic weapons to undermine America.

The fourth realization is that Putin has clearly been courting the Chinese to work with Russia in attacking the dollar. In fact, Putin repeatedly urged the so-called BRICS nations (Brazil, Russia, India, China, and South Africa) to act together to undermining the dollar's reserve currency status.[239] We have ample evidence that this is the case, dating back to 1998 with Russian efforts to join Russia, India, and China in an alliance to challenge the United States.[240]

In May 2012, Pravda reported very boldly that Russia was urging China to join forces against the West.[241] In March 2013, the Christian Science Monitor echoed those thoughts with the headline, "With US-Russia relationship toxic, Moscow looks to strengthen ties with China." According to this article,

> China's new President Xi Jinping chose Moscow, where he arrived Friday for a three-day visit, to be his first foreign destination, highlighting strengthening ties between China and Russia . . . underlying that is a growing sense that the two countries are being driven together by shifting geopolitical winds, which are alienating each from the West while intensifying the need for more reliable partnerships. As Xi arrived in Moscow Friday, Mr. Putin stressed that ties

between Russia and China have never been stronger, and they are set to grow warmer still.

'Our relations are characterized by a high degree of mutual trust, respect for each other's interests, support in vital issues. They are a true partnership and are genuinely comprehensive,' Putin told the official ITAR-Tass agency.

'The fact that the new Chinese leader makes his first foreign trip to our country confirms the special nature of strategic partnership between Russia and China,' he added."[242]

Assuming that Putin failed in his attempt to get China to join Russia in attacking the American economy in 2008, can we be certain that a repeated effort would be rebuffed? Prior to the financial crisis of 2008, the total U.S. federal debt was in the $9 trillion range. At the time of China's President Xi Jinping's visit to Moscow, that debt had risen to nearly $17 trillion. It is now approaching $20 trillion. There should be little doubt that our vulnerability to such an attack has increased sharply. The fact that Putin's Russia became the world's largest buyer of gold, with China as the next runner up only adds to the concern. Journalist Gwynn Guilford wrote in a 2013 article:

> Russian President Vladimir Putin has been loading up on gold. As Bloomberg reports, the Russian central bank has amassed 570 metric tons of it in the last 10 years, making it the biggest global gold buyer.
>
> Why is Russia's central bank betting on gold rather than holding its foreign reserves in something with a bit of yield? It's a hedge against a collapse in the value of one of the global reserve currencies. 'The more gold a country has, the more sovereignty it will have if there's a cataclysm with the dollar, the euro, the pound or any other reserve currency,' Evgeny Fedorov, a lawmaker for Putin's United Russia party, told Bloomberg."
>
> Russia's not the only one that's been hoarding gold, though. China is the next runner up, having added one-quarter less than Russia, according to Bloomberg.
> 243

Keep in mind that in 2009, Panarin reiterated his claims that the U.S. economy would collapse and be replaced by global leadership from Russia and China.[244] Their gold buying combined with direct statements from both calling for the dollar's demise match almost precisely with what you would suspect from nations prepared to use external economic weapons. Couple all of that with Sejna's revelations of KGB strategy, and the Chinese *Unrestricted Warfare* writings, and a clear pattern appears.

In October 2013, the official Chinese news agency seemed to echo Putin, calling for the world to be "de-Americanized" and an end to the use of the dollar as the world's reserve currency.[245]

In March 2014, Voice of Russia quoted U.S. investor Jim Sinclair in what appeared to be a direct warning to America:

> Russia is fully in control of the petrodollar and could cause the Dow Jones industrial average to plummet as it has never done before. One can wave the Stars and Stripes as long as one likes, but it's a fact that the Russians can turn the US economy upside down.[246]

A few weeks later, *Voice of Russia* offered the headline "Russia prepares to attack the petrodollar."[247] From then until now we have seen a steady state of cooperation between Russia and China that appears aimed at the dollar-based Western financial system.

REPLACE THE IMF, REPLACE THE DOLLAR?

It is increasingly apparent that Putin believes that the world is locked in a global economic war and is planning for Russian victory. His perception was seemingly validated when the IMF and the European Union joined in an effort to confiscate a percentage of all deposits over 100,000 euros in Cyprus bank accounts.[248] Cyprus has been a banking haven for Russians and it was widely perceived that this effort was targeted at them.[249] The IMF, in particular, is viewed as a U.S. instrument of power.[250]

Shortly after the actions in Cyprus, the BRICS nations announced plans to develop their own development bank to rival the IMF and the World Bank. According to a 2013 RT.com report,

> The move is linked to the developing world's disillusionment with the status quo of world financial institutions. The World Bank and IMF continue to favor US and European presidents over BRICS nations, and in 2010, the US failed to ratify a 2010 agreement which would allow more IMF funds to be allocated to developing nations.
>
> The BRICS have called for a reconstruction of the World Bank and IMF, which were created in 1944, and want to put forth their own 'Bretton Woods' accord. And they are serious. "Brics is not a talk show. It is a serious grouping," Zuma told reporters at the presidential guest house in Pretoria. The new bank will cater to developing world interests and will symbolize a great economic and political union. "There's a shift in power from the traditional to the emerging world. There is a lot of geo-political concern about this shift in the Western world,"

Martyn Davies, chief executive officer of Johannesburg-based Frontier Advisory, told Bloomberg.[251]

At the same time, the BRICS nations also began to discuss ways to replace the U.S. dollar as the currency used for global trade. An initial $30 billion per year deal has already been struck between China and Brazil in conjunction with the BRICS efforts. According to a 2013 International Business Times article:

> By shifting some trade away from the U.S. dollar, the world's primary reserve currency, the two countries aim to buffer their commercial ties against another financial crisis like the one that resulted from the collapse of the U.S. housing market bubble in 2008. [252]

China has already replaced the United States as Brazil's primary trading partner, an amazing development over the past few years. With Putin's encouragement, this will be the first of multiple efforts to make the United States less relevant. On a combined basis, the BRICS already rival the American economy with $14 trillion in annual economic activity.[253] Even India appears enthusiastic about this possibility, according to the International Business Times.

> "We are creating new axis of global development," Anand Sharma, India's Minister of Commerce, Industry and Textiles, Xinhua reported. "The global economic order created several decades ago is now undergoing change and we believe for the better . . ."[254]

Following the initial rumblings at the BRICS summits, we have seen a very systematic approach to developing a full-fledged alternative to nearly every aspect of the Western system.

First, we have seen the creation of the Asian Development Bank. Supported by Russia, the Chinese created an institution that could rival the World Bank. Initially, the Obama administration response was to ignore the bank and encourage our allies to do the same. Chinese influence apparently was greater, however, as one by one our closest allies joined the effort.[255] Even former Treasury Secretary Larry Summers admitted that this single development might mark the end of American economic leadership in the world.[256]

Then, we saw the development of CIPS (the China International Payment System) as an alternative to SWIFT (the Society for Worldwide Interbank Financial Telecommunication system). When transactions occur between two countries, they typically travel through the SWIFT system. While the SWIFT system is privately held, it has been the subject of American pressure to achieve geopolitical objectives. A recent example was cutting off Iran with international sanction prior to the 2015 nuclear deal with Iran. Historically, such a move was tantamount to economic isolation. Putin greatly feared that Russia might one day be cut off and thus pursued two strategies. The first was to get Russia on the board of SWIFT, something achieved in early 2015. Second, Russia supported Chinese efforts to create a viable alternative, the China International Payment System. ZeroHedge explained the purpose of this effort in a 2015 article.

> One of the recurring threats used by the western nations in their cold (and increasingly more hot) war with Russia, is that Putin's regime may be locked out of all international monetary transactions when Moscow is disconnected from the EU-based global currency messaging and interchange service known as SWIFT (a move, incidentally, which SWIFT lamented as was revealed in October when we reported that it announces it "regrets the pressure" to disconnect Russia).

> Of course, in the aftermath of revelations that back in 2013, none other than the NSA was exposed for secretly 'monitoring' the SWIFT payments flows, one could wonder if being kicked out of SWIFT is a curse or a blessing, however Russia did not need any further warnings and as we reported less than a month ago, Russia launched its own 'SWIFT'-alternative, linking 91 credit institutions initially. This in turn suggested that de-dollarization is considerably further along than many had expected, which coupled with Russia's record dumping of TSYs [U.S. Treasury securities], demonstrated just how seriously Putin is taking the threat to be isolated from the western payment system. It was only logical that he would come up with his own.

> There were two clear implications from this use of money as a means of waging covert war: 1) unless someone else followed Russia out of SWIFT, its action, while notable and valiant, would be pointless - after all, if everyone else is still using SWIFT by default, then anything Russia implements for processing foreign payments is irrelevant and 2) if indeed the Russian example of exiting a western-mediated payment system was successful and copied, it would accelerate the demise of the Dollar's status as reserve currency, which is thus by default since there are no alternatives. Provide alternatives, and the entire reserve system begins to crack.[257]

CIPS has been successful in attracting multiple international banks.[258] At the same time, SWIFT has lost some of its luster with recent revelations of successful hacking attempts against the system.[259] Undermining SWIFT through hacking serves only to strengthen CIPS.

Even as CIPS begins to gain prominence, China and Russia are intent on proving that global trade can take place without involving American dollars. From 2014 to 2015, ruble-yuan settlements increased by over 800%.[260] China has used this as a roadmap to expand local currency settlement with other trading partners.[261] All of this has led to growing internationalization of the yuan. Clearly, all of these developments have led to one of Putin's greatest desires – seeing the yuan added as a legitimate global reserve currency by the IMF.

Having the yuan as a fully convertible global reserve currency would allow Russia to eliminate dollar holdings if it so chose. Russia could also conduct international transactions away from a U.S.-led system. And Moscow could access capital either through the IMF or the Asia Development bank. In short, Russia could eliminate the need for dollars and encourage other nations to follow suit, thus ending American economic hegemony. Perhaps this is why we have seen a global reduction in holding US Treasury bonds.

The implications for the United States are immense. A Russia-China alliance is quite formidable. Even the U.S. Defense Department recognizes this. [262] A successful dethroning of the dollar as primary reserve currency would prove catastrophic for the American economy. Without reserve status, it is unlikely that foreigners would be willing to fund our huge debt, for example. Putin knows this and recognizes that the economic warfare strategy concocted by the Soviet Union and later alluded to by Igor Panarin could indeed prove decisive in defeating America.[263]

ENERGY: ANOTHER FRONT IN THE ECONOMIC WAR

Of course, currencies and banking are just one front in the economic war. Energy is the most important sector of Russia's economy and the rapid growth of American energy production based on hydraulic fracking in shale formations has the potential to change everything. For one thing, it can tip the trade balance and dramatically strengthen the dollar. This clearly works against Putin's efforts to dethrone America's economy. No wonder experts view Russia the big loser in regard to fracking. Associated Press reporter Kevin Begos wrote in September 2012:

> The Kremlin is watching, European nations are rebelling, and some suspect Moscow is secretly bankrolling a campaign to derail the West's strategic plans. It's not some Cold War movie; it's about the U.S. boom in natural gas drilling, and the political implications are enormous.

> Like falling dominoes, the drilling process called hydraulic fracturing, or fracking, is shaking up world energy markets from Washington to Moscow to Beijing. Some predict what was once unthinkable: that the U.S. won't need to import natural gas in the near future, and that Russia could be the big loser.

"This is where everything is being turned on its head," said Fiona Hill, an expert on Russia at the Brookings Institution, a think tank in Washington. "Their days of dominating the European gas markets are gone."

Any nations that trade in energy could potentially gain or lose.

"The relative fortunes of the United States, Russia, and China – and their ability to exert influence in the world – are tied in no small measure to global gas developments," Harvard University's Kennedy School of Government concluded in a report this summer.[264]

Knowing what we know about Vladimir Putin, it is abundantly clear that he would not take these developments lying down. And he hasn't. It is well documented that Putin has publicly opposed fracking of any type. Russia's Gazprom is on record claiming that shale gas development is harmful to the environment. Under normal circumstances and with many heads of state, this would be viewed as political posturing. In the case of Russia and Putin, however, these pronouncements are reflective of their strategy.

It has been documented that the KGB funded environmental groups to further Soviet policy. It seems likely that such efforts have continued under former KGB officers Putin and Panarin. According to Oleg Kalugin, former Head of Counterintelligence for the KGB,

> The environmental movement was also targeted for KGB infiltration, he says, with the simple message that the best way to preserve nature was to work against the system that would exploit it for profits . . .
>
> Kalugin says the new regime in Russia is not to be trusted, and that Americans must be on their guard.[265]

This is significant due to the fact that something as simple as declaring a single lizard to be endangered has the potential to shut down energy development.[266] In the case of the Permian basin, the loss could have been as much as 500 million barrels of domestic oil. Fortunately, despite serious pressure from environmental groups, the Department of Interior chose not to declare the Sand Dune Lizard endangered, allowing the Basin to produce almost two million barrels per day by 2016.[267] [268] Some might believe it absurd to imagine that a two-inch lizard could prevent the production of two million barrels of oil per day, valued closed to $200 million at present.

The Heritage Foundation documented how the UAE funded a Matt Damon movie designed to turn American opinion against fracking.[269] Their motive is simple and obvious. It is not a stretch to believe that other major energy producers such as

Russia would likewise fund efforts designed to stop American efforts to expand oil and gas production.

Of course, efforts to stop fracking can also go far beyond funding of the green movement. In the case of Poland, a promising area for natural gas shale development, some believe that Putin had a role in a 2010 plane crash that devastated a pro-fracking government. [270]

In addition to Russia, China has reason to curtail American energy development. According to a 2012 CNBC.com article, cheaper access to energy could revive the U.S. manufacturing sector and pose a real threat to Chinese growth.

> With oil production at a twenty-year high and predictions of a manufacturing renaissance for the U.S. economy, one of the world's largest investment banks has detailed how the "shale revolution" will negatively affect emerging markets such as China . . .
>
> With the help of cheap energy, manufacturing will pick up and move down the ladder to capturing the production of less "sophisticated" goods (computers, fabricated metals and automobiles) currently manufactured in emerging nations. As a result, the United States will likely compete with emerging markets for market share rather than being a consumer, Morgan Stanley said ...
>
> Brazil could also suffer, with a Mexican economy that's closely knitted to the U.S. attracting more automobile manufacturing, [according to the Morgan Stanley report.]
>
> [The report also said that] U.S. reindustrialization will likely challenge Russia's presence in steel, chemicals and industries to support that very renaissance.[271]

Does this reality explain why there has been a dramatic ramp-up of Chinese hacking attempts against North American energy companies? Of course, the Russians and Chinese were not alone in a desire to derail the American energy boom. In late 2014, the Saudis made it plain that they intended to undermine American energy production. Their approach was to ramp up production and drive prices lower until the fracking companies failed. Many believe that this move was designed to target Russia and Iran as well. After all, Russia needs an even higher price per barrel to survive than our domestic shale industry. Some estimate they need $110 per barrel to meet budget obligations over the long term.[272]

Amazingly, despite the serious drop in the price of oil, Russia has survived and Putin has retained popularity. Even more surprisingly, the Russians have found a basis to begin developing ties with Saudi Arabia.[273] As the United States has warmed to Iran, the Saudis may see a need to attract Russia and draw closer to China. This is very significant because an axis between Russia, China, and the Saudis could clearly challenge the American dollar.

CYBER WARFARE, ATTACKS ON THE STOCK MARKET, AND THE ULTIMATE ECONOMIC WEAPON

Russian cyber capabilities are well known. Yet, few realize that the Russians have already hacked the NASDAQ infrastructure that is so critical to our stock market. In fact, according to press reports, they placed a "digital bomb," presumably to sit undetected until a time of their choosing.[274] Recall how a Russian national was convicted in 2013 (although later acquitted) of stealing trading algorithms from Goldman Sachs. Goldman thought that this action was a serious risk to their firm and presumably the markets.[275] Even if the taking of the codes was innocent, the fact that they could be taken so easily is real. And, the reality that stolen trade codes could destabilize the market is frightening.[276] In the wake of the "flash crash" of 2010, we must admit that our markets are vulnerable. A Congressional briefing in 2010 made this point clearly.[277] General Keith Alexander confirmed this when he was NSA Director in a 2013 *60 Minutes* interview.[278]

In addition to the NASDAQ hack, we have definitive proof that Russian spies have been researching methods for destabilizing our stock markets. In fact, a banker acting as spy was arrested in January 2015 after the FBI eavesdropped on a conversation with his Russian handler telling him to explore how Exchange-Traded Funds and 'trading robots" could be used to destabilize American stock markets.[279]

All of this is a part of a very sophisticated cyber strategy to undermine America's reputation and the American economy. Russia has some of the world's best hackers.[280] Most recently, the Russians have been blamed for hacking the Democrat National Committee (DNC) and accused of attempting to influence the 2016 election. Russians also have been blamed for cyber attacks on the State Department and even the White House.

Although the Obama administration had been reluctant to fully attribute blame or forcefully respond to this alleged Russian hacking, this changed in the summer of 2016 due to Wikileaks hacks of the computers of the Democratic National Committee and Hillary Clinton's campaign. On October 11, 2016, the administration formally announced Russia was behind the Wikileaks hacks. That same day, in a joint press release, the Director of National Intelligence and Department of Homeland Security said the two agencies "were consistent with the methods and motivations of Russia-directed efforts." Obama and Clinton campaign said meant U.S. intelligence agencies had determined Russia was behind these hacks. (Which it had not done, at least not publicly.) Obama officials later said the United States would conduct a "proportional" cyber response to alleged Russian hacking of Democratic Party computers.[281]

Pressure on the Obama administration to retaliate against the Russian hacks grew in October 2016 after Wikileaks began to release thousands of mails of Clinton campaign members. While many of these emails were highly embarrassing to the Clinton campaign, they received little press attention.

What is worse is that Russia has apparently weaponized cyber for use in military conflict as well. As just one example, Russia is widely suspected to have used cyber weapons to take down the Ukrainian power grid. According to a January 2016 Bloomberg.com article:

> A successful cyber-attack on a power grid is a nightmare that keeps intelligence services and security experts awake at night. Now the threat is no longer theoretical: A grid in Ukraine has been brought down by hackers. The vulnerability they used? As so often with hacking, human stupidity.[282]

The engineered blackout scenario is so scary that Ted Koppel, the former ABC *Nightline* host, recently published a book about it. In "Lights Out: A Cyberattack, A Nation Unprepared, Surviving the Aftermath," Koppel claimed the U.S. is unprepared for an attack on one of the three power grids that distribute electricity throughout the country. He wrote:

> If an adversary of this country has as its goal inflicting maximum damage and pain on the largest number of Americans, there may not be a more productive target than one of our electric power grids.[283]

Ukraine has an adversary that may be interested in inflicting just such damage and pain: Russia.

Taking down the power grid may be the ultimate weapon in economic warfare. Cyber is one means of accomplishing this devastating attack. An electromagnetic pulse (EMP) weapon is another. Regardless of the cause, a long-term power grid outage (a year of longer) would be a nation-ending event, as noted by Dr. Peter Pry and Ambassador James Woolsey in a 2014 *Wall Street Journal* op-ed:

> In a recent letter to investors, billionaire hedge-fund manager Paul Singer warned that an electromagnetic pulse, or EMP, is "the most significant threat" to the U.S. and our allies in the world. He's right. Our food and water supplies, communications, banking, hospitals, law enforcement, etc., all depend on the

electric grid. Yet until recently little attention has been paid to the ease of generating EMPs by detonating a nuclear weapon in orbit above the U.S., and thus bringing our civilization to a cold, dark halt . . .[284]

What would a successful EMP attack look like? The EMP Commission, in 2008, estimated that within 12 months of a nationwide blackout, up to 90% of the U.S. population could possibly perish from starvation, disease and societal breakdown.

In 2009, the congressional Commission on the Strategic Posture of the United States, whose co-chairmen were former Secretaries of Defense William Perry and James Schlesinger, concurred with the findings of the EMP Commission and urged immediate action to protect the electric grid. Studies by the National Academy of Sciences, the Department of Energy, the Federal Energy Regulatory Commission and the National Intelligence Council reached similar conclusions."[285]

CONCLUSION

There is no doubt that Russia currently has very sophisticated economic weapons at its disposal, ranging from nation-ending options such as EMP and cyber to market manipulation, energy warfare, and currency warfare. The Russians personally know the power of economics and have studied and planned for economic warfare dating back to the KGB and the Soviet Union. Vladimir Putin appears particularly attuned to both the nuances and capabilities of economic conflict.

The Unsolved Mystery Behind the Act of Terror That Brought Putin to Power*

By David Satter

All available evidence points to Putin's complicity in the 1999 apartment-building bombings in Russia. Those who have tried to investigate have been killed off, one by one.

I believe that Vladimir Putin came to power as the result of an act of terror committed against his own people. The evidence is overwhelming that the apartment-house bombings in 1999 in Moscow, Buinaksk, and Volgodonsk, which provided a pretext for the second Chechen war and catapulted Putin into the presidency, were carried out by the Russian Federal Security Service (FSB). Yet, to this day, an indifferent world has made little attempt to grasp the significance of what was the greatest political provocation since the burning of the Reichstag.

I have been trying to call attention to the facts behind the bombings since 1999. I consider this a moral obligation, because ignoring the fact that a man in charge of the world's largest nuclear arsenal came to power through an act of terror is highly dangerous in itself.

Russian human-rights defenders Sergei Yushenkov, Yuri Shchekochikhin, Anna Politkovskaya, and Alexander Litvinenko also worked to shed light on the apartment bombings. But all of them were murdered between 2003 and 2006. By 2007, when I testified before the House Foreign Affairs Committee about the bombings, I was the only person publicly accusing the regime of responsibility who had not been killed.

The bombings terrorized Russia. The Russian authorities blamed Chechen rebels and thereby galvanized popular support for a new war in Chechnya. President Boris Yeltsin and his entourage were thoroughly hated for their role in the pillaging of the country. Putin, the head of the FSB, had just been named Yeltsin's prime minister and achieved overnight popularity by vowing revenge against those who had murdered innocent civilians. He assumed direction of the war and, on the strength of initial successes, was elected president easily.

Almost from the start, however, there were doubts about the provenance of the bombings, which could not have been better calculated to rescue the fortunes of Yeltsin and his entourage. Suspicions deepened when a fifth bomb was discovered in the basement of a building in Ryazan, a city southeast of Moscow, and those who had placed it turned out to be not Chechen terrorists but agents of the FSB. After these agents were arrested by local police, Nikolai Patrushev, the head of the FSB, said that the bomb had been a fake and that it had been planted in Ryazan as part of a training exercise. The bomb, however, tested positive for hexogen, the explosive used in the four successful apartment bombings. An investigation of the Ryazan incident was published in the newspaper Novaya Gazeta, and the public's misgivings grew so widespread that the FSB agreed to a televised meeting between its top officials and residents of the affected building. The FSB in this way tried to demonstrate its openness, but the meeting was a disaster: It left the overwhelming impression that the incident in Ryazan was a failed political provocation.

Three days after the broadcast, Putin was elected. Attention to the Ryazan incident faded, and it began to appear that the bombings would become just the latest in the long list of Russia's unsolved crimes.

In April 2000, a week after Putin's election, I decided to go to Ryazan. The residents of 14–16 Novoselov Street, where the bomb had been planted, were suffering from heart problems and depression, and their children were afraid to go to sleep at night. Those I met were completely convinced that the incident had not been a training exercise. "Who can imagine such a thing?" asked Vladimir Vasiliev, whose initial reports of suspicious activity had led to the arrest of the FSB agents. "But the claim that it was a test makes no sense. Does it make sense to test people for vigilance at a time when the whole country is in a state of panic?"

Two motions in the Duma to investigate the Ryazan incident failed in the face of monolithic opposition from the pro-Putin Unity party. In February 2002, a third motion to investigate failed and a group of Duma deputies and human-rights activists organized a "public commission" to seek answers independently. Its chairman was Sergei Kovalyev, a Duma deputy and former Soviet dissident. Sergei Yushenkov, another Duma deputy, was the vice chairman. The commission had no official standing, but the Duma deputies could pose questions to the government in their individual capacity.

By 2002, the commission members were facing a rising tide of indifference. The second Chechen war was being prosecuted successfully and an economic boom was gaining momentum. Putin's popularity rose to an all-time high.

Shortly after the commission began its work, however, an incident occurred that reminded Russians of just how mysterious the apartment bombings were. In March, the newspaper Noviye Izvestiya announced the result of its investigation into the fact that Gennady Seleznev, the speaker of the Duma and a close associate of Putin, had announced the bombing in Volgodonsk on September 13 – three days before it occurred. Vladimir Zhirinovsky, the head of the Liberal Democratic Party, told journalists that same day what Seleznev had said, but they could not confirm it, so it was not reported. On September 16, however, the building in Volgodonsk really was blown up, and on September 17 Zhirinovsky demanded an explanation of how Seleznev had known about the bombing in advance.

"Do you see what is happening in this country?" he said, shouting and gesticulating from the podium in the Duma. "You say an apartment building was blown up on Monday and it explodes on Thursday. This can be evaluated as a provocation." Seleznev avoided responding, and Zhirinovsky had his microphone turned off when he persisted in demanding an explanation.

In March 2002, however, Noviye Izvestiya succeeded in obtaining the transcript of what Seleznev had said on September 13, 1999. His precise words were: "Here is a communication which they transmit. According to a report from Rostov-on-Don today, this past night, an apartment house was blown up in the city of Volgodonsk." The newspaper asked him who had informed him about the bombing in Volgodonsk three days before it happened. He answered, "Believe me, not [exiled oligarch Boris] Berezovsky," who had accused Putin of orchestrating the bombing. In this way, he indicated that he was well aware of who, in reality, had given him the information.

Seleznev then told the newspaper that, on September 13, he had been referring to an explosion on September 15 that was part of a war between criminal gangs and had not claimed any victims. Seleznev's explanation, however, raised more questions than it answered. It was hard to understand why such an insignificant incident needed to be reported to the speaker of the Duma at a time when apartment buildings were being blown up, with hundreds of deaths. And even if Seleznev had been referring to a minor criminal conflict in Volgodonsk, how was it possible that he had been informed about it two days in advance?

A new source of accusations against Putin and the FSB emerged in London. Berezovsky, who had been instrumental in facilitating Putin's rise to power but then had gone into exile after being deprived of his influence, held a press conference on March 5, 2002, in which he accused the FSB of carrying out the bombings with Putin's complicity in order to justify a second Chechen war.

The apartment bombings took place while Putin was prime minister and the head of the FSB was Nikolai Patrushev, his longtime protégé. But the planning for such a complex operation would have had to begin much earlier, before Putin became prime minister, at a time when Berezovsky was one of the most powerful members of the leadership. Berezovsky played a critical role in Putin's ascent, making the case to members of the Yeltsin entourage that Putin should become prime minister. Berezovsky's attitude toward Putin changed only when Putin acted to remove him from power. Berezovsky began to hint and then, in December 2001, to state openly that the apartment bombings had been carried out by the FSB, with the complicity of Putin.

Putin could hardly respond to Berezovsky's accusations by saying that the real initiator had been Berezovsky and that he himself had been just a passive participant. Putin was later to accuse Berezovsky of responsibility for every major political murder and terrorist act that took place in Russia, but, in regard to the apartment bombings, he had to remain silent. In the words of the Russian publicist Andrei Piontkovsky: "The more hopeless became [Berezovsky's] chances of returning to the political arena in Russia, the louder became his accusations. . . . It seems that he opened a completely new form of political business: Blackmail the authorities with the exposure of one's own crimes."

The independent commission began its work in February 2002 and achieved one important success. Yushenkov and Duma deputy Yuli Rybakov flew to London to attend the March 5 press conference organized by Berezovsky. Yushenkov met fugitive former FSB agent Alexander Litvinenko, who introduced Yushenkov to Mikhail Trepashkin, a former FSB agent and orthodox Communist who had been fired by the FSB after investigating the links between FSB officers and Chechen organized crime. After this meeting, Trepashkin began cooperating with the public commission.

In April 2002, Yushenkov traveled to the U.S., where he met Aliona and Tanya Morozov, whose mother had been killed in the 1999 explosion in Moscow's Guryanova Street. The Morozov sisters were officially crime victims, which meant they could present evidence in court proceedings. Tanya Morozova agreed to give Trepashkin her power of attorney, allowing him to submit evidence on her behalf.

The person who rented the basement on Guryanova Street where the bomb had been placed had been using the passport of Mukhid Laipanov, a resident of the Karachaevo-Cherkesiya republic in the North Caucasus. The real Laipanov, however, had been killed in an auto accident in February 1999, seven months before the bombing took place. The police said that his passport had been used by Achemez Gochiyaev, an ethnic Karachai and the director of a Moscow construction firm.

In the immediate aftermath of the Guryanova Street bombing, the police interviewed Mark Blumenfeld, the building superintendent. His description of the person who had rented the basement apartment was used to create a police sketch of a suspect. The sketch, however, was then quickly replaced with one of Gochiyaev, who looked completely different. When Gochiyaev learned that he was being accused of blowing up a building, he went into hiding.

At the end of March 2002, Yuri Felshtinsky, a historian and an associate of Litvinenko, received a call from someone who said he was acting on behalf of Gochiyaev. At the end of April, an intermediary turned over a handwritten statement from Gochiyaev in which he said that he had been set up and had fled only because he knew that the FSB was getting ready to kill him. Trepashkin found Gochiyaev's testimony convincing and decided to concentrate on locating the sketch of the original suspect.

On the night of April 17, 2003, I was working in my Moscow apartment when I received a call telling me that Sergei Yushenkov had been shot dead in front of the entrance to his apartment building. My book *Darkness at Dawn*, in which I argued that the FSB was responsible for the apartment bombings, was due out in the U.S. in May, and now Sergei, who held the same view, had been murdered.

Sergei was an active member of the public commission and had been full of enthusiasm when a few months earlier he had told me of plans to expose the real story of the bombings. I got up and went to the window and looked at the surrounding buildings, the street lamps, and the all-but-empty street. What horror is going on in this country? I wondered. For the first time in the 27 years I had been writing about Russia, I felt afraid even to leave my apartment.

Yuri Shchekochikhin, another member of the public commission, died three months later. He was the victim of a mysterious illness that caused his skin to peel off and his internal organs to collapse. The Russian authorities refused to allow an autopsy, but his relatives managed to send tissue samples to London; based on these samples, he was tentatively found to have died from thallium poisoning. Thallium is the substance also believed to have been used in the poisoning of Roman Tsepov, Putin's former bodyguard, in September 2004.

Shchekochikhin had been a friend of mine since the 1980s. Shortly before his death, he presented me with a copy of his latest book, *Slaves of the KGB: 20th Century, the Religion of Betrayal*, about persons forced to work under the Soviet regime as informers. Yuri inscribed it: "We are still alive in 2003!"

With the deaths of Yushenkov and Shchekochikhin, Trepashkin was the only person left actively investigating the apartment bombings. As the lawyer for Tanya Morozova, he was entitled to review the FSB file, and he began to search for the original sketch of the suspect. He went through the file carefully but could not find any picture, suggesting it had been removed from the file.

Acting on a hunch, Trepashkin began going through old newspaper archives in the hope that the original sketch had been published somewhere before the FSB had pulled it from circulation. After an exhaustive search, he finally found it. To his surprise, it was a sketch of someone he knew: Vladimir Romanovich, an FSB agent who in the mid-1990s had been responsible for investigating Chechen criminal organizations.

Trepashkin next began to search for Blumenfeld, who was identified in the file as the person who had provided the description. He found Blumenfeld, who agreed to talk to him. Blumenfeld said that on the morning of the bombing he had described to the police the man who had rented the basement space, and that two days later he had been taken to Lefortovo prison, where FSB officers pressured him to change his story and "recognize" a photo of a different man, Gochiyaev.

Trepashkin now was in a position to discredit the official explanation of the bombings, which Viktor Zakharov, the head of the Moscow FSB, had given in September 2000. Zakharov had said: "We know the entire chain. . . . The direct organizer of the terrorist acts was . . . Gochiyaev, known in Chechnya under the nickname 'The Fox.' He also led the perpetrators of the terrorist acts. All of them are adherents of the radical current of Wahhabism." A trial was being prepared for Yusuf Krymshamkhalov and Adam Dekkushev, two members of what the authorities were calling the "band of Gochiyaev" who allegedly transported explosives to Volgodonsk.

Trepashkin was preparing to present the evidence based on the rediscovered original sketch and Blumenfeld's claims in court, but first he connected Blumenfeld with Igor Korolkov, a reporter for Moskovskiye Novosti. Blumenfeld confirmed to Korolkov that "the man publicly presented by the investigation as Gochiyaev was not in fact Gochiyaev."

"In Lefortovo prison," Blumenfeld also said, "they showed me a photograph of Gochiyaev and said I had rented the basement to him. I said I never saw this man. It was insistently recommended to me that I identify Gochiyaev. I understood everything and ceased arguing."

On the day after his meeting with Korolkov, Trepashkin was arrested and his apartment was searched. He was then accused of improper use of classified material and was sentenced to four years' imprisonment in a labor camp in the Urals. As a result, his important testimony was never presented as evidence in court.

With the arrest of Trepashkin, the investigation of the apartment bombings faltered. Those in Russia who wanted to raise the issue lacked investigative tools such as subpoena power and were well aware that too active an interest could cost them their lives. The rest of the world was complacent, unwilling to consider the implications of a terrorist's being in charge of the world's largest nuclear arsenal.

In May 2003, Darkness at Dawn was published. A month later, I presented the book in Washington at the Hudson Institute, where I am a senior fellow. A German film crew arrived with Aliona Morozova. I explained why I believed that the apartment bombings were a provocation. My remarks provided the central narrative of a film titled "Disbelief," which premiered in 2004 at the Sundance Film Festival. A Russian-language version of Disbelief was put on YouTube and circulated widely in Russia.

But, unfortunately, real action required civic leaders — and persons capable of helping to make the bombings a serious political issue were disappearing one by one. Anna Politkovskaya, Russia's leading investigative journalist, and Alexander Litvinenko continued to speak out on the case. Politkovskaya was shot dead in the elevator of her apartment block on October 7, 2006; Litvinenko died on November 23 from radioactive polonium-210 that had been put in his tea in a London sushi restaurant.

When I moved to Russia to work as an adviser and contributor to Radio Liberty in September 2003, I had no immediate plans to deal with the apartment bombings. But I knew the subject would arise eventually. I believe that the Russian authorities were aware of this, too. In fact, the apartment bombings are impossible for a conscientious observer to ignore. The circumstantial evidence that the bombings were carried out by the FSB is overwhelming. The only reason there is no direct evidence is that the Putin regime has concealed it. In the case of the Ryazan incident, the authorities have sequestered the persons who put the bomb in the basement, the records of the exercise, and the dummy bomb itself. They putatively did this to protect state secrets, but, according to Russian law, among the things that cannot be considered state secrets are facts about "catastrophes threatening the security and health of the citizens" and "violations of the law by state organs and officials."

The greatest barrier to accepting the evidence that points to the FSB as the perpetrator of the bombings is sheer reluctance to believe that such a thing could be possible. By any standard, murdering hundreds of innocent and randomly chosen fellow citizens in order to hold on to power is an example of cynicism that cannot be comprehended in a normal human context. But it is fully consistent with the Communist inheritance of Russia and with the kind of country that Russia has become.

Russia never really forgot the apartment bombings. During the anti-Putin protests in 2011 and 2012, demonstrators carried signs referring to the attacks. It is common in Russia for people to avoid certain issues because otherwise "it will be impossible to live." Unfortunately, an issue doesn't disappear simply because it is ignored. Of all the dangers that hang over Russia, none is more menacing than the failure to demand answers to the 17-year-old mystery of how Putin came to power.

Russia's New Information War: What It's Like and What to Do About It

By J. Michael Waller

Russia's new information war is a logical outgrowth of the way Vladimir Putin engineered his rise to power. As the security minister and designated successor to the ailing and alcoholic President Boris Yeltsin in 1999, Putin engineered the bombings of apartment buildings in southern Russia and blamed the slaughter on Chechen rebels. His "propaganda by deed" provided the pretext to launch a new war to smash the Chechen rebellion. Both created the mass outrage that called for strong and decisive leadership, manufacturing and focusing public demand his quiet ouster of Yeltsin on the night of Y2K.

Seen through that lens, the Kremlin's weaponization of information is a logical, proven, cost-effective means of domestic political action, internal security, and international power projection. It succeeds because neither the Russian public nor the West demanded a public accounting of Russia's Communist past the role of the former KGB as the sword and shield of the Soviet state. Both were willing to suspend their belief for their own purposes.

Inaction from three successive American presidents empowered Putin and unwittingly gave the otherwise weak Russia an enormous capability to wage war, sometimes without firing a shot. Information, properly applied, gives leverage to the materially weaker side. The Kremlin's new information warfare and propaganda capabilities, while innovative for a government, merit concern mostly because of the West's flaccid and delayed response.

The capabilities and actions present a strategic challenge. With the grave but unsurprising exception of subversion of the U.S. political system, they hardly merit the breathless reportage and commentary from many political observers, because they have been building up visibly for more than a decade.

Putin's unnecessarily aggressive info-centric actions give the U.S. and its partners the pretext to exploit the potentially profound vulnerabilities of the secret-police regime, and the fragilities that, if exploited, could widen many existing splits within the Putin leadership itself and the Russian Federation at large.

All this, of course, lowers the threshold of conflict to the level of classical espionage, propaganda, and subversion, at which the Kremlin has excelled for the past century, with a modern digital twist. The U.S. and its allies generally have opted not to engage, out of the quaint "gentlemen don't read other people's mail" principle, or more likely, simple ignorance about what to do or how. After a long period of not wanting to see, the West finds itself surprised and alarmed at being on the receiving end of what historically is a simple and manageable method of statecraft.

PROPAGANDA, INFORMATION WARFARE, AND INFORMATION WAR

Different but complementary methods define Russia's information war. The first is propaganda: the content of messaging and other communications methods to influence and manipulate the perceptions, thought processes, opinions, beliefs, and ultimately actions of target audiences. Propaganda includes deeds meant to be seen (or perhaps unseen) for the same purposes. "Disinformation," a literal translation of the Soviet-era Russian word dezinformatsiya which refers to deliberately false information, is an element of propaganda. For decades, the U.S. has liked to pretend that only its enemies and adversaries engages in or should engage in propaganda. For that reason, and with some exceptions, the U.S. has done its own propaganda poorly or not at all, and never quite grasped the essence of how its adversaries do it – and how best to counter it.

Properly done, propaganda is waged in concert with other methods of persuasive communication like diplomacy, public diplomacy, journalism, education, marketing, entertainment, and other messaging to influence perceptions and attitudes. Those methods are executed most effectively through subversion of institutions and values, and advanced for calculated psychological effect to shape cognition within the human brain. They also are carried out through political action and political warfare to provide direction and move the targets toward the perpetrator's desired outcomes. This combination is summarized in a magnificent Soviet portmanteau of agitation and propaganda into the official Communist Party term "agitprop."

Elements of these actions include what the Russians call provokatsiya, or "provocation," to manufacture incidents that justify action in a predetermined direction, or to goad a domestic or foreign opponent into making a self-defeating action or reaction. An extreme form of provokatsiya was the series of apartment bombings in Moscow, Buynaksk, and Volgodonsk in September 1999 that killed 293 and injured more than a thousand people. Investigative journalists found beyond doubt that the FSB internal security service, which Putin headed as minister of security and first deputy prime minister, planted the bombs in the high-rises. The bombings provided the pretext Putin needed to push Yeltsin from power.

Russian political culture, as expected, birthed a splendid term for this spectrum of conflict – agitation, propaganda by word, propaganda by deed, provocation, disinformation, and controlled violence – literally translated as "active measures."

Today's Russian political and security culture, then, is steeped in a century or more of its own words that create their own universe of thought and deed. The U.S. has no similar terms of its own origination, because it never was seriously in the game.

"Propaganda" was common and official term in Soviet tradecraft. But the Putin regime recognizes the limitations among Western audiences, and the idea that only the bad guys do it. In today's Russia, propaganda is bound by its own limits. What the Kremlin used to call propaganda, it now calls "information war." This is an important change for practical reasons beyond the aesthetic: the Machiavellian and nationalist Putin revived the concept that politics is war, information is a weapon of war domestically, and that his regime can wage this type of war externally in what the West still considers peacetime. Information war of the Russian strain is not to be confused with "information warfare" of the American variety.

In the West, information warfare is the use of computers and other information systems to disrupt or destroy targets within or alongside a kinetic military conflict. Many in the U.S. will differ with this definition based on their responsibility or perspective, or due to confusion about the meaning among competing authorities in the military. But the fact is that the official term did not exist before the digital age. Information warfare can include the neutralization or destruction of civil communications or military C3I networks, banking and financial systems, navigational systems, energy power grids, and logistics and supply chains through electronic or physical manipulation of information systems. The military terms "cyber warfare" and "information operations" are components of information warfare. This is mainly the 1's and 0's of digital communication and processing, and the flow of electrons in software that operate computing, sensory, and mechanical systems. This chapter pays little attention to cyberwar capabilities as understood in the West. The point is that Russia under Vladimir Putin has shown a new and creative capability in the propaganda and information warfare spaces, combining elements excellent Soviet tradecraft with modern tools and methods.

REINFORCING PUTIN'S PERSONAL POWER BASE

Russia's new offensive capabilities for waging both propaganda and information war abroad occurred as Putin built a cult of personality around himself domestically to be the only viable leader of Russia. Building that cult required stamping out most independent news and information for the domestic population.

The process meant doing away with Russia's unfinished experiment with objective reality, and manipulating reality, as Orwell warned in *1984*, into something new and contrived. That meant manipulating the past to shape the future, and controlling the present to control the past. To keep the regime in power, which was the purpose of seizing it in the first place. One of the most distinguished surviving observers of Putin's rise amid the apartment bombings, journalist David Satter, encapsulated how Russians look at their past in the unusual title of his book, "It Was a Long Time Ago, and It Never Happened Anyway." His latest work about the Putin era captures the mentality today: "The Less You Know, The Better You Sleep."

Which brings us back to the information war. Putin combined domestic propaganda with enforcement mechanisms to impose self-censorship and to destroy the viability of any threats to his political power. His regime built an information warfare capability used on at least two major occasions to date to launch cyber attacks on foreign sovereign governments that Moscow believes should remain part of its historically entitled space, as one would launch a military attack but without provoking a kinetic response. It also built a modern cyber espionage capability to spy on domestic and foreign targets, and use the products of that espionage for propaganda and political warfare purposes at home and abroad.

Building those capabilities coincided with a centralization and personalization of political authority in Russia, to further weaken the already weak federal system by appointing regional governors instead of allowing citizens to elect them, and to suck economic wealth from the regions to finance the central regime. As the ultimate enforcement, Putin used domestic intelligence collection for propaganda purposes to destroy his opponents politically, financially crippled them so they would flee Russia for good, co-opted them internally through positive incentives or neutralized them through intimidation, physically incarcerated them through selective criminal prosecution.

The most stubborn holdouts wound up dead through gangster-style hits in St. Petersburg apartment stairways or driveby-style shootings on a bridge to Red Square, targeted hit-and-run "accidents," aviation malfunctions, bombings, poisoning by chemical and exotic polonium radiation, defenestration, and old-fashioned blunt-force trauma. These assassinations not only eliminated opponents; they were propaganda-by-deed in modern Russia's information war to spread the word about crossing the boss.

WHAT HAPPENED TO THE OLD SOVIET GLOBAL NETWORKS

Old Communist networks are effectively gone. Russia no longer maintains the old Soviet Communist Party (CPSU) overt and semi-overt active measures networks of controlled party organizations and international front groups. The command-and-control system, CPSU Central Committee International Department, long disappeared, though some of their younger functionaries (and their adult children, trained for the purpose) remain active. Those Communist parties and fronts, with national units around the world, were means of coordinating and executing action-oriented Soviet active measures campaigns globally. Their organization embraced specific themes, such as peace and disarmament, youth and students, clergy and laity, organized labor, women, Afro-Asian solidarity, and national self-determination.

The Moscow-funded national communist parties whose controlled cadres ran the host-country chapters of those fronts have largely evaporated or morphed into different parties and movements in their respective countries. Recruitment efforts for younger successor personnel are believed to have died out.

KGB and its successors survived. While the old Soviet Communist Party front organizations are gone or ineffective, the covert machinery and tradecraft of the KGB, a state institution, survived. Soviet leader Mikhail Gorbachev reluctantly split the KGB into separate services in late 1991, and Russian President Boris Yeltsin preserved them along with their *Chekist* bureaucratic culture. Yeltsin resisted calls to abolish or purge the old KGB services, reveal their past crimes, or establish civil oversight mechanisms, and there was no pressure from the U.S. and other democracies for him to do so.

The KGB's active measures division, Service A, sat within the KGB First Chief Directorate for foreign intelligence, as was Service S to handle "illegals" operating under deep cover, and the service for handling recruited agents among citizens of targeted countries, including and especially the United States. The First Chief Directorate spun off intact and un-reformed in late 1991 to become Russia's present External Intelligence Service (SVR). In addition to espionage, the SVR continues to run influence operations worldwide through controlled agents in mainstream news organizations, business, religious organizations, universities and think tanks, political parties and movements, official government positions, and private companies that contract their services to the government.

The FBI and CIA no longer issue unclassified reports for the public and Congress about Russian influence campaigns (nor did Congress call for those agencies to issue them), so little is public about this issue from the U.S. intelligence community. The community often leaked or openly commented about the aggressive nature of Russian espionage, characterized as being as intensive, if not more, as at the height of the Cold War. But Western counterintelligence services, apart from a short-lived experiment after 2001, generally did not perform the full field of their missions. They concentrated on counterespionage – against spies who steal secrets – but rarely against agents of influence. They did not appear to collect or analyze much intelligence on Putin's information war, and are not known to have targeted SVR assets for propaganda and disinformation, until about 2015. This blind area presents a combination of "known unknowns" and "unknown unknowns" that stymies a solid assessment of Russian propaganda, information war, and subversion, and how to build proper countermeasures, defenses, policies, and doctrines. Fortunately, enough open source material exists to develop a strong public understanding.

Legacy information outlets. Most Soviet-era information and media outlets were privatized or simply assumed by different investors, groups, political parties, or businesses. Some dramatically transformed. New ones spun off or emerged. Some of the most important, including TASS and RIA-Novosti, remained. Consistent with an attitude to keep the past in the past, TASS kept its cryptonym, which stands for Telegraph Agency of the Soviet Union. The RIA-Novosti network claimed lineal descent from Stalin's Soviet Information Bureau, but after the Soviet collapse, RIA-Novosti enjoyed a reputation as an excellent source of quality journalism. The old government ministry to control the press remains as the Ministry of Communications and Mass Media.

Russia's new media – a mix of the privatized Soviet legacy outlets and new independent outlets – competed for audiences either through paid advertising or some sort of subsidy, usually from a business network or oligarch who either genuinely supported of a free press or, more commonly, used media holdings as weapons of economic and political power. The Russian media offered lively, interesting, and generally uncontrolled news and entertainment for practically everyone, with a few outstanding publications and programs that flourished with world-class reporting.

Given his career as a KGB internal security liaison with the East German Stasi, and the nature of his murderous agitprop that justified his rise to power, Putin saw freedom of information as a threat to his own personal and political security. Preparing to remove or eliminate any potential rival, Putin began to close in on Russia's media organizations in 2004, while hiring American and European public relations firms to plant positive stories in the Western press.

RUSSIA'S CENTRALIZED, DECENTRALIZED MEDIA MACHINE: TO ELEVATE PUTIN AT HOME AND ABROAD

The crown jewel of Moscow's media machine is an information group called Rossiya Segodnya (Russia Today). The domestic and international satellite television and multimedia conglomerate emerged from preparations for the country's 2006 presidential campaign and Putin's quest to make Russia great again.

Presently the order of battle works like this: Alexei Gromov, Putin's deputy chief of staff, coordinates the official government line to Russian editors. Reporting to Gromov, the All Russia State Television and Radio Broadcasting Company, under direct Kremlin control, owns Russia Today, with programming in Russian, English, Arabic, Spanish and other languages now under the RT brand. Most other media are concentrated under direct state control, or indirectly through parastatal entities like the Gazprom natural gas conglomerate, or coopted oligarchs.

Russia Today was the brainchild of Michail Lesin, an engineer-turned-advertising tycoon who became Yeltsin's spinmaster during the 1996 re-election. Lesin's story is an important indicator of the nature of Putin's information war machine.

Lesin served as press and mass communications minister as Putin readied to ease Yeltsin out of the presidency in 1999. Putin retained the imaginative and aggressive state media chief, nicknamed Bulldozer, to destroy political opponents and build the Russian leader's cult of personality.

Under Lesin, Russia's experiment with free media began to close. Lesin used government power to control or physically take over Russia's media through a combination of cash payments and privilege, extortion, forced or fraudulent purchases of independent news companies and their property, and outright theft. He transferred prominent media enterprises to Gazprom Media, the information division of the colossal natural gas company that Putin would ultimately revert to state control. Lesin pulled the Yeltsin-era licenses that had allowed Radio Liberty and the Voice of America to broadcast on commercial stations inside the country, effectively silencing most U.S.-sponsored programming as RT established its U.S.-based operations.

These and other measures would elevate Putin's public stature as the country's unchallenged – and unchallengeable – leader. There could be no alternative.

Journalists devoted to freedom of the press had little future. Some bowed with the prevailing winds, went into business, or fled the country. *Novaya Gazeta* editor and investigative journalist Yuri Shchekochikhin, who went into politics, aggressively probed official government corruption and the 1999 apartment bombings. He was scheduled to travel to Washington in 2003 to meet with the FBI about his findings, and died a painful death by poisoning. Authorities denied the family a medical report, and forbade foreign forensic examiners to test the body tissue. Investigative reporter Anna Politkovskaya, who antagonized Putin with the same type of reporting as Shchekochikhin but from the ground in and around Chechnya, received death threats, survived a 2004 poisoning attempt, and withstood a mock execution at the hands of Russian soldiers. Finally she was shot dead in her Moscow apartment on October 7, 2006, Putin's 54th birthday. (FSB defector Alexander Litvinenko, in London, accused Putin of assassinating Politkovskaya and said that he had urged the journalist to escape from Russia. On November 1, Litvinenko developed symptoms similar to those of Shchekochikhin and died of radiation poisoning weeks later.)

Meanwhile, Putin had been re-elected with 71 percent of the vote in 2004. He elevated Lesin as an unofficial superminister of propaganda, making him a "special adviser" on media affairs and reputedly granting him almost at-will presidential access. In that capacity, Lesin inspired the 2005 creation of Russia Today, which would later rebrand itself as RT.

With RT running strong, Lesin became chief of Gazprom Media in 2013, the cash-rich company that gobbled up and operated the television stations taken from the opposition. His brash manner alienated him from many Russian elites, and the Bulldozer finally had a falling out with Putin the next year. He abruptly left Gazprom Media in 2015, went on his own to California and Washington, D.C., where his story ended.

On a Washington evening that November, Lesin failed to appear at a fundraiser for the Woodrow Wilson Center for Scholars. Two days later, in the 1950s-ish Dupont Circle Hotel, a custodial worker found Lesin's dead body. Before District of Columbia authorities began the autopsy, state-controlled Russian media reported that the 57 year-old former Putin insider had died of natural causes. RT announced passively, "It has been reported that Lesin had been suffering from a prolonged unidentified illness."

A D.C. medical examiner autopsy later revealed that Lesin was killed from blunt-force trauma to the head, and the body suffered blunt-force trauma to the neck, limbs, and abdomen.

RUSSIA TODAY/RT

Russia Today launched in 2005 as a multimedia public diplomacy channel to offer "Russia's view," presenting a fresh, young face to the world. An early intent was to become a peer of the Qatar-owned Al Jazeera global cable news network.

RIA-Novosti named a politically loyal 25-year-old as Russia Today's director, jumping over a generation of experienced journalists and message-makers to staff the new operation with people mostly under age 30. Russia Today hired scores of young and inexperienced foreign journalists, mostly British at first, paying them six-figure salaries and generous benefits for relatively little work.

The channel limped along until Moscow's 2008 war against the Republic of Georgia. Its nearly exclusive access to Russian combat forces and officials in Moscow made the channel indispensable for anyone following the military campaign. (In another dimension of Russia's information war development, that war included a massive cyber attack against Georgia, a repeat of the attack on Estonia's cybergrid the year before.) Still, Russia Today struggled for the desired international viewership. The collapse in oil prices that year forced the Kremlin to tighten its belt almost across the board, but Russia Today proved itself a value play.

Though directed from the Kremlin, Russia Today staff also had freedom, within boundaries, to innovate from the bottom. It became clear that the world audience had little interest in news about Russia. The combination of cynicism within Russian politics and journalism as a whole, big perks for youthful and inexperienced writers and staff, and the proliferation of global social media enabled the regime accomplish its purposes by appealing to angry and cynical audiences on all edges of the political spectrum.

No longer would the Kremlin's trendiest outlet be Russia's "voice" around the world, in terms of covering Russian affairs or sending a coherent message from Moscow. With exceptions, Kremlin direction would not be in the form of an old Soviet-style party line designed to convince and mobilize audiences. The power of suggestion would be sufficient enough for most Russia Today writers and announcers. The simple editorial line was simple. Play up the extreme as the new normal. Hack away at the West. Do nothing to undermine Putin. Seek to deepen growing foreign audiences' often justified frustrations and fears about their own governments, institutions, leaders, and societies. And accept the occasional tactical orders and meddling from Moscow Center.

To look less Russian, Russia Today repackaged the name of its channels to RT. It marketed itself with bright hipster graphics, urging English- and Spanish-speaking audiences to "question more."

This change occurred just before Secretary of State Hillary Clinton pushed the famous "re-set" button in 2009. Soon, RT began outperforming more established satellite and Internet channels. Russia Today strove to become unconventional and outrageous in its English-language programming. It sought an openly sexy array of young presenters, with edgy graphics and special effects. From a new, advanced studio and production facility in Washington, D.C. with a staff of 100, RT began more in-depth, serious reporting on American society. It became the most popular foreign television channel in most U.S. cities. As it built its market share, RT reverted to its antagonistic, anti-U.S. tone, portraying itself as the anti-CNN. By 2010, RT expanded its global staff to 2,000, with new channels in Arabic and Spanish, with others planned.

As Russia's economy sagged and its standing in the world declined during the "reset" period, RT became more antagonistic and cynical. Programming goaded Europeans to question their American ally, and for RT's growing American viewership to question their own country. RT heralded the Edward Snowden defection and scandal-mongered the National Security Agency (NSA), fueling the first widespread suspicion of to Moscow was the most dangerous U.S. intelligence service. RT pushed conspiracy theories again, alleging that the Russian-born Islamist terrorists behind the Boston Marathon bombing were part of a U.S. government plot. Washington might be responsible for the Ebola virus, RT hinted, and the Ukrainian government deserved blame for the shoot down of Malaysia flight MH17.

Putin rewarded his unconventional investment. He multiplied RT's annual budget tenfold, from $30 million in 2005 to $300 million in 2013. That year, in a trophy move, RT hired the dated but iconic American news talk host and CNN veteran Larry King.

RT built a global audience of 700 million. Its social networks enjoy 3.8 million Facebook supporters in English, 2.8 million in Spanish, and more than 10 million in Arabic. In 2013, with 1.5 million subscribers to its YouTube channel, RT became the first TV channel to get one billion views on Google's video platform. Indirect viral distribution RT's English, Spanish, and Arabic programming appears in three million hotel rooms worldwide. After briefly considering belt-tightening measures amid government budget cuts, Putin boosted RT's 2016 budget to $415 million.

Deftly expanding its online presence in the declining and atomized global media sector, RT built a market share to become what more of its fans consider to be a somewhat mainstream online news service. Soviet propaganda outlets never reached such audiences. On its way to becoming the un-CNN, RT created an online wire service, Sputnik, designed ultimately to become a peer to Reuters. Sputnik News generally takes a more balanced line than RT, appearing more credible. Unlike RT, whose reporters and bureau chiefs are frequently countermanded from Moscow, As of this writing, Sputnik is decentralized. Its local editors say they are free to publish what they want, though they admit in private that they are mindful of who pays them.

In Washington, Sputnik America presently has a staff of eight, some of whom are veteran journalists and scholars who say they could find no other employment amid the collapsing media business. They crank out a heavy output, with each writer producing an average of five short articles per day. That amounts to an impressive 40 well-written pieces a day from the Washington bureau alone, or about 200 monthly. The Washington office does not employ highly paid, young, left-wing hipsters. It hires rather poorly paid, older, experienced reporters with little other opportunity in the collapsing American journalism sector. Several Sputnik writers are politically conservative, some with a long documented record critical of Moscow. Sputnik America hired at least four individuals who had been contractors for an online U.S. military psychological operations program, and lost their jobs after Congress cut off funding.

GENERAL THEMES AND TARGET AUDIENCES

The new thematic approach has worked. Soviet political propaganda targeted left-wing and soft-left audiences in a controlled setting, with soft propaganda channeled through compromised or fully recruited agents of influence Western journalists, academics, think tank experts, and politicians into the mainstream.

RT has built what has been called "a largest cult following on the fringes of the left and right in the West." Indirect viral distribution improves RT's credibility because friends and affinity groups validate the RT message by passing it along to those who trust them. By prompting people to "question" what they are told, RT appeals to critical thinking while producing a stream of content that encourages precisely the opposite.

Through Moscow-funded NGOs, the Kremlin has funded extreme causes in the West that RT then denounces as a "fascist revival" to discredit Ukraine and frontline NATO allies.

Targets: Frustrated and angry people. RT's English-language programming appeals to North American and European audiences on the left, as well as environmentalists, anti-globalists, libertarians, nationalists, conservatives, right-wingers, and sectors of the financial elite. It plays on their often legitimate suspicions and fears of their own governments, the European Union superstate in Brussels, and of the centralized overreach of U.S. leadership and security agencies. The information network also targets conservative Christians who hold traditional moral and social values at a time when the political and cultural leadership in their societies drift further from them, or – even more important for RT's purposes – that impose objectionable practices as matters of social pressure, policy, and law.

The propaganda strategy is paired with a subversive strategy of funding anti-establishment, patriotic or nationalist political parties, movements, and leaders. This activity extends to the United States, to undermine public confidence in political and constitutional institutions. In contrast to the left-wing activists for unilateral disarmament who publicly denied Moscow funding and direction during the Cold War active measures campaigns, some of their opposites in the RT fan club rationalize or defend the Kremlin connection today. Many, it appears, seem unaware of RT's ties to the Russian government. Calls are rare to keep their causes pure from Kremlin cooptation, as was the case when Islamist regimes and agents infiltrated conservative as well as progressive groups and movements. In the U.S., mainstream conservatives (including the Drudge Report) and libertarians often circulate RT content as part of their news diet, giving the Kremlin further reach and credibility.

RT tries to evoke an eclectic, perverted libertarianism and diversity of traditionalism without true respect for either. Sputnik says that its mission is to "point the way to a multipolar world that respects every country's national interests, culture, history and traditions."

Blended into its high-volume, frequently contradictory, and often overwhelming content, RT promotes extremist fringe elements from both sides of the Atlantic, passing them off as mainstream or at least authoritative. Former NSA contractor Edward Snowden, who defected to Moscow under FSB control, and his collaborator, WikiLeaks founder Julian Assange, are free speech "victims." Holocaust denier "Ryan Dawson" is portrayed as a human rights activist. Neo-Nazi Manuel Oschenreiter is hosted as a "Middle East analyst," and so on.

RT accuses Western societies of restricting freedom of speech in the name of security, while pointing to Russia's few irrepressible journalists to show how free media flourishes under Putin. Its director, Dmitry Kiselev, had once been a junior Soviet international propaganda bureaucrat. He now portrays himself not as a propagandist but as an "abstract journalist," and a victim of Western democracies who is "the first and so far the only journalist to be targeted by coordinated E.U. sanctions."

"East and West appear to be trading places," Kiselev wrote in a 2014 London *Guardian* op-ed.[286] "In Russia we now take full advantage of freedom of speech, whereas in the West political correctness, or political expediency in the name of security, have become arguments against freedom of speech." Kiselev's message resonates with Westerners justifiably fearful about centralized political and economic power, and erosion of their freedoms under the rubric of security.

RT created what has been called a clash of narratives to confuse audiences and sow greater doubt and anger in order to "exacerbate divides and create an echo chamber of Kremlin support," according to a 2015 report by the Institute of Modern Russia.[287] According to the report, the effect is not to persuade, as with public diplomacy, or even to be considered credible, "but to sow confusion via conspiracy theories and proliferate falsehoods."

Objective truth is absent in RT, another contrast to the Soviets claimed to have their own version of objective reality. "Even if they were lying they took care to prove what they were doing was 'the truth,'" said Gleb Pavlovsky, who had worked on Putin's election.[288] "Now no one even tries proving the 'truth.' You can just say anything. Create realities." Pavlovsky should know. "I first created the idea of the Putin majority – then it became real. Same with the concept of there being 'no alternative' to Putin," he said.

In a fully Orwellian way, the Putin regime is creating new realities through its peacetime information war. Domestically, as before, the cynical Russian public pretends to believe and is rewarded with content that appeals to their cynicism. Back in Soviet times, military doctrine posited quantity being a quality of its own. The same theory holds true with Putin's information war doctrine. RT emphasizes sheer mass of information over journalistic integrity. A 2016 Rand Corporation study called RT and the entire state media model a "firehose of falsehood."

"The aim of this new propaganda is not to convince or persuade, but to keep the viewer hooked and distracted, passive and paranoid, rather than agitated to action. Conspiracy theories are the perfect tool for this aim," according to the Institute of Modern Russia report which also noted that "linguistic practices aimed at breaking down critical thinking" help keep cognitive functions passive."

Russia Today's model proved so successful that the Kremlin authorized it to take over the respected RIA-Novosti news service and the international Voice of Russia radio.

ONLINE REACH

The Internet makes it easier than ever for the Kremlin to spread its influence worldwide through all the obvious means. To add some nitrous oxide to its high-octane information machine, Moscow has adeptly exploited social media and established a strong and growing market share. As with the rest of RT, the goal is not to persuade, but to lower the quality of debate, discourage rational discussion, intimidate others, and frustrate legitimate journalists.

With high-paced, intensive online production of entertaining and emotional content, Russia creates its own reality; there is no need for fact-checking of multiple sourcing as with real journalism. Objective reality matters little. First impressions matter most. Multiple sources thus spread similar message, with quantity substituting for quality. The sources earn multiple "likes" or endorsements, and get passed along, boosting reader acceptance, with reinforcement from the recipients' peer groups. Items of relatively little interest in terms of volume rely on trusted experts to legitimize them. Items that prove to be popular build credibility through the frequency with which they are "liked" or otherwise legitimized, and passed along. Repetition begets familiarity. Familiarity begets acceptance.

Army of trolls. To attack opposing views online, Moscow has built its own army of Internet trolls. A troll is someone who posts comments online to disrupt, provoke, or otherwise ruin reasonable discourse. Many trolls are simply troubled individuals. Some companies, political groups, and governments hire people to act as trolls to attack their opponents. The Kremlin's information war effort has raised its own virtual army. According to a former Russian paid troll, Moscow hires troll cadres to operate 24 hours a day, seven days a week, in 12-hour shifts, with a daily quota of posting 135 comments of at least 200 characters each.

Trolling is done in concert with Russian military objectives. A scientific Latvian study of Russian trolling in support of its military objectives in Ukraine and against NATO found that Moscow seeks "to create confusion and mistrust" among its target audiences in a giant online psychological warfare campaign.

HUMAN INFLUENCE APPARATUS AND NETWORKS

As in Soviet times, the Putin regime attempts to co-opt Western influencers by providing them with special access in exchange for cooperation, and denying access and prestige to those who won't play along. "Other senior Western experts are given positions in Russian companies and become de facto communications representatives of the Kremlin," Peter Pomerantsev and Michael comment in their study, providing specific examples that include prominent political and business figures. Subsequent to that study, the U.S. Congress instructed the intelligence community to collect on these efforts. Moscow funds think tanks to divide NATO member states from one another, the alliance as a whole, and the United States. Public relations companies like Ketchum in New York operate on a paid consultancy basis to serve as covert and overt propaganda placement agents in the Western media.

Though not controlled in the sense of a recruited agent, these influencers – in journalism, academia, think tanks, politics, government, culture, religion, and business – temper any criticism and exaggerate praise in order to maintain special access and treatment in Russia, and to build or keep the prestige and value that comes with that access.

Privatization of state property, and the warfare among bureaucrats and oligarchs for the spoils, reached an equilibrium under Putin, who brought the strategic industries and most powerful oligarchs into line and under state control, or at least domination. The Kremlin utilized them to finance political influence operations around the world. The tricks relied on the subtlety of using state control to provide or deny access, grant simple preferential treatment for doing business in Russia, post leading Western political and business figures on the boards of major Russian businesses, and to place Russians on the boards of Western companies. They also involved targeted Russian investment in Europe and the United States, to subsidize, leverage, or even bail out businessmen of political importance.

To temper the attitudes of Western leaders in business, journalism, academia, and politics, Putin created the prestigious Valdai Forum as an annual gathering to meet top Russians, including the president himself. The Kremlin uses the Valdai Forum to grant privilege to foreign figures of influence who in turn increase Putin's prestige at home and abroad, and to tame experts by making them fear losing access and professional stature. The public pattern fits the old Soviet KGB pattern of cultivating foreign individuals to serve as witting or unwitting agents of influence, as described in a captured KGB training manual from the late Soviet period. But the pattern ranges on a larger scale through oligarchs dependent on the regime leadership.

Meanwhile, Moscow maintains and expands its inherited Soviet network of controlled agents of influence around the world, including in the United States. Not much is publicly known about them today, but if Soviet precedent is an indicator, they would be nationals of their own countries, or Russian émigrés, as well as third-country nationals including Americans, recruited to act in any position of influence.

DISINFORMATION, FAKES AND FORGERIES

Moscow revived the Soviet-era use of disinformation, fakes and forgeries, but this time on an accelerated level through electronic media. A study published in an Estonian military journal examined more than 500 instances of Russian falsehoods with 18 main narratives that accompanied the military campaigns against Ukraine in Crimea and the Donbass. State-controlled Russian media took advantage of democratic rhetoric by passing off the disinformation as simply a different point of view.

Quality varies, but the fakes and forgeries appear in such volume, generating high concentrations of stories online, that they overwhelm any efforts to expose and discredit them. Even so, a variety of nonprofit or volunteer groups has emerged, mostly in Ukraine and frontline NATO countries, to document and expose the forgeries and press for government capabilities to counteract them.

ESPIONAGE-DRIVEN PROPAGANDA

Effective strategists worldwide have collected intelligence for the purpose of using it as propaganda, but Moscow has long excelled at the art for both domestic and foreign purposes. The U.S. and its allies generally no longer do. Empowered with cybertools and online outlets, Putin raised the stakes.

Internally, Russian regimes have used kompromat, the exploitation of compromising situations and information, to blackmail, blackball or discredit certain opponents. Most kompromat is done quietly to make the target acquiesce. Before he took power, Putin pioneered kompromat for TV purposes to destroy targets in public. As Yeltsin's security chief, he had a state-controlled television channel broadcast covert camera footage of Prosecutor General Yuri Skuratov in a sexual tryst. Skuratov had been working with the Swiss to investigate corruption of Yeltsin's family members. The kompromat-on-TV setup finished Skuratov's career.

RT creator Mikhail Lesin, then head of the All-Russia State Television and Radio Broadcasting Company, helped prepare Putin's FSB footage of Skuratov for public viewing. That operation is believed to have cemented Lesin's relations with Putin, and caused Yeltsin to reward Lesin with the cabinet position as press minister in 1999. Kompromat-for-TV provided the perfect edgy, entertainingly scandalous platform to inject the destructive intelligence into the mainstream for domestic political purposes, and to intimidate others into submission.

Internationally, Russian intelligence went beyond RT to steal information and release it, perhaps for the purposes of kompromat (we do not know for a fact), but certainly to disrupt, demoralize, discredit, and divide political and social institutions in other countries. The United States has been the prime target.

First came WikiLeaks, founded in 2005 – the year after Putin's decision to weaponize information – which calls itself an "international journalistic organization" devoted to the anonymous posting of classified information for all the world to see. WikiLeaks exploited public frustrations and fears with restrictive, overarching, and often poorly-conceived security measures during the Global War on Terror. It exposed colossal quantities of classified information, mainly from U.S. government agencies, complicating American relations with other countries and damaging Washington's image at home and worldwide. WikiLeaks, and its apparently independent image, encouraged frustrated U.S. government employees and contractors, among others, to download classified information for universal online publication.

It remains to be seen whether WikiLeaks and its Australian founder, Julian Assange, set out to be, or unwittingly became, controlled assets of the Russian government, but drawing distinctions is only a legalistic exercise. Seasoned counterintelligence authorities recognize an agency relationship with the Russian services. Regardless, WikiLeaks and Assange were instrumental in enabling the defection of disgruntled NSA contractor Edward Snowden to Russia in 2013 after stealing a vast amount of classified data, from the U.S. government. The low-level Snowden may have had help in choosing what types of electronic data to select and steal. Assange and Snowden frequently appeared on RT to denounce the United States and its powers at home and abroad. For the purpose of mapping the Russian information war, WikiLeaks and those who feed into it are important tools.

WikiLeaks appears to be an outward manifestation of Russia's espionage-driven propaganda, not only through insider theft and leaks, but through sophisticated hacking into classified U.S. government information systems, state government systems, and private data systems. Westerners tended to mirror-image such hacking as attempts to collect intelligence for the purpose of informing decision makers. The Russians view hacking as not only that, but as a normal part of information war – not merely in the "information warfare" cyber sense, but in the sense of spying for the purpose of agitprop.

From what the American public was told during the last months of the 2016 presidential campaign, Russian or Russian-backed hackers broke into state electoral database in what authorities termed an attempt to manipulate the elections. The hackers stole internal data from the Democratic National Committee (DNC) and party organizations, reporters from the *New York Times* and other news organizations, think tanks, and other entities involved in shaping U.S. public opinion, policy, and leadership. WikiLeaks published more than 20,000 internal DNC emails, prompting the abrupt resignation of the party chairwoman.

The effort must have been massive. U.S. officials reported that Russia's Federal Security Service (FSB) and its GRU military intelligence service were caught doing their own separate hacking operations of the campaigns of Hillary Clinton and Donald Trump, and pro-Republican political action committees. The cyber attacks on Republicans received less publicity and did not surface through WikiLeaks. The hacked private emails of former secretary of state Colin Powell, among others, became public. Whether the FSB is indeed engaged in such action instead of, or in addition to the SVR, or Moscow's FAPSI analogue to the NSA, is not publicly known.

FBI advance warnings of the hacks prompted many who had been blind to cyber security or foreign espionage to suddenly become counterintelligence-conscious Russia hawks. The issue quickly became politicized, degenerating along partisan lines during the presidential campaign. The revelations added an extra bitter and too-late-to-prove set of issues of the already toxic political atmosphere. The perfect timing and conditions further fueled suspicions and motivations of each of the two major presidential nominees, with Assange promising an "October surprise" just before the election. Major mainstream news organizations raised the possibility that Russia's espionage-driven propaganda was designed to aid Republican nominee Trump against Democrat candidate Clinton. This possibility morphed into a widely presumed, if unproven, fact. With symphonic echo-chamber effect, RT gleefully reported on the new aspect of an already ugly campaign.

The U.S. leadership failed to respond effectively to the FBI warnings. Apart from angry diplomatic words, it lost the opportunity to turn the tables by preparing accurate material from the vast amounts of intelligence collected on the corruption and other foibles of Putin and his inner circle, sanitizing it, and releasing it in-kind. Such an action could have had an equalizing effect and served to deter future espionage-driven political warfare.

The FBI warned election officials in all 50 states of Russian hacking threats to manipulate voting records and election results. The Departments of Justice and Homeland Security unwittingly fueled public fears further by offering to intervene at the federal level to "protect" the state- and local-controlled electoral systems. Clinton, with no public record of hawkishness against aggressive Russian espionage, pounced on her opponent, slamming Trump in the final presidential debate as a "Russian puppet."

'CURIOUS INCIDENT:' THE DOG THAT DIDN'T BARK

U.S. officials probably became aware of the strategic design and intent of Russian propaganda and information war in 2015, when a marginalized former member of Putin's inner circle came under federal investigation for money laundering after buying multimillion-dollar real estate properties in California. That individual was Mikhail Lesin, the Putin image-maker and media mogul who conceived of RT and the new strategy of information war.

By then marginalized and certainly aware of the grim fates of others with guilty knowledge, Lesin visited Washington in November, 2015. He was believed to be talking to the FBI to make a deal. He disappeared for a couple days before being found in his Dupont Circle Hotel room, dead from blunt-force trauma to the head and neck.

The violent death, just blocks from the White House, of a once-trusted Putin insider now in trouble with the FBI, ordinarily would have any Kremlin information warrior, to say nothing of any good investigative journalist. The strangest part of Lesin's unsolved murder is not Moscow's suspected role. The strangest part was that the violent death of the creator of RT never became a Russian propaganda theme.

Somehow, RT and other state-controlled outlets "knew" within hours of the discovery of the body that Lesin had died of natural causes due to a long illness brought on by excessive drinking and smoking. Anyone who knew Lesin would find that to be a logical cause of death.

For nearly a century, "died after a long illness" has been a staple of Kremlin propaganda to explain away inconvenient deaths. Shortly after news of Lesin's demise, a Kremlin spokesman issued a statement saying that Putin "highly appreciates the enormous contribution Mikhail Lesin made to the formation of the modern Russian media."

In perhaps the first public report of the Bulldozer's demise, RIA Novosti cited an un-named "family member" saying that Lesin "died from heart stroke." TASS sourced an anonymous Russian Embassy official in Washington who supposedly said that "police found no signs of foul play." RT simply quoted from those multiple and apparently mutually-confirming reports.

The Russian Foreign Ministry claimed to know nothing. But District of Columbia medical examiners, apparently wary of the deaths of other particularly knowledgeable Putin foes, seemed to be looking for high-tech assassin's chemicals in Lesin's body tissues, or the extremely rare polonium-210 isotope used to assassinate Litvinenko in London. Four months later, after a long silence during exhaustive tests, D.C. authorities released the forensic information that revealed something different. The Bulldozer had died from massive blunt-force trauma to the head and neck. Officials did not state how the trauma occurred, but noted that the torso and extremities showed signs of similar trauma. With the news of the violence of Lesin's death now public, the Russian Embassy in Washington blamed U.S. authorities for providing no information.

The media outlets that Lesin had created or directed reported on the autopsy results, but cast doubt on any Russian involvement. Some hinted that the U.S. government murdered Putin's former confidant, saying that "conspiracy" stories about a hidden Russian hand were a deliberate "false lead." RT quoted a writer for the *Executive Intelligence Review* as an authority floating the "false lead" story, implying that the publication was somehow connected to the U.S. intelligence community when it is in fact a discredited journal published by the fringe Lyndon LaRouche organization.

In its unfashionable 1950s glass-and-yellow-brick curved building, the Dupont Circle Hotel is updated and trendy, but considered "relatively downscale" and a far cry from the lifestyle of high-flying Russians. It would be an odd place for Lesin to have preferred to stay. The hotel's rates, though, are within the ossified per diem structure of the FBI, with its limited funds to support defectors from abroad. Lesin may have been talking to the FBI to prevent his prosecution and to be allowed to remain in the U.S.

Was Lesin indeed murdered as it appears? If so, by whom? There is no clear answer. The Washington, D.C. police stated in 2016 that "the incident remains an active Metropolitan Police Department investigation." RT continued to discount any foul play. The Russian Embassy added nothing to its complaint alleging a lack of information.

The silence indicates that someone at the top of the Kremlin told the controlled media not to make a big deal about Lesin's death, leaving them to the predictable default position of implying that the Americans might have done it. Sherlock Holmes creator Arthur Conan Doyle might have termed the silence a most "curious incident." In his 1892 mystery "Silver Blaze" about a stolen race horse and murder of its trainer (also from blunt force trauma to the skull), Holmes deduced the perpetrator by what did not happen: the guard dog that didn't bark. In solving the mystery, Holmes mentioned "the curious incident of the dog in the night-time." But, responded another detective, "The dog did nothing in the night-time."

"That was the curious incident," said Holmes. "Obviously the midnight visitor was someone whom the dog knew well."

WEAK U.S. RESPONSE

Part of Putin's propaganda and information war success has been the weak response of the United States and NATO. The West did little to discourage the crackdown on free news and entertainment media in Russia or support the independent media meaningfully. Washington did nothing when the Kremlin put the squeeze on traditional U.S.-sponsored media like Radio Liberty and the Voice of America, while it permitted Putin's own information war machine to grow inside the United States. The U.S. failure to press Moscow on Lesin's apparent murder gave added propaganda benefit to Putin of showing, as with Litvinenko in London, that the West cannot protect defectors from harm.

OPTIONS/RECOMMENDATIONS

The United States needs to re-learn how Moscow waged active measures in the past, and learn how it has refined those methods to the information age today. Policy options are endless. As a first start, U.S. leaders must carry out the following inexpensive and rapid actions that are relatively easy to do with the proper strategy, people, and authority:

- Show Moscow that two can play that game:
    - Collect, process, sanitize, and release selective intelligence to the public on key members of Putin's present inner circle and family to expose corruption and other crimes, and personal behavior that is unacceptable to Russian culture.
    - Develop a calibrated divisive strategy to exploit: (1) internal fissures within the Putin inner circle and regime; (2) tensions within economic and industrial sectors in Russia and abroad that are vital to the survival of that regime; (3) political and economic tensions between the centralized power of Moscow center and the Russian regions; (4) regional, ethnic, linguistic, and cultural tensions that, if exacerbated, could cause the dissolution of the Russian Federation in a manner similar to the collapse of the Soviet Union.
    - Prepare and execute the above strategies when necessary.
- Use the presidency as a megaphone, the way President Reagan did against the Soviets, to expose Russian information war strategies and practices, and mandate every relevant executive agency to do the same.

This will condition people to be alert for Russian information war, and lessen the impulse or the need to refute every message.

- Start a new presidential administration with a clean slate.
    - o Deny political clearances and appointments to any individual who willingly participated in Russian state-controlled propaganda activities since 2004.
    - o Instruct U.S. officials not to grant access to, or interviews with, any Russian state-controlled media;
    - o Deny political or policy access to any individual or organization that willfully participated in Russian state-controlled propaganda activities since 2004.
    - o Deny U.S. government contracts, grants, and clearances to any individual or company that willfully participated in any Russian state-controlled propaganda activity since 2004.
    - o Encourage leaders of Allied and partner countries to do the same.
- Use existing law to impose reciprocity on Russian state-controlled media, by matching Moscow's squeezing off U.S. government-funded RFE/RL and VOA with a reciprocal U.S. squeeze of Kremlin-funded media in the United States.
- Empower the FBI to monitor and apprehend U.S.-based, Russian government-controlled, agents of influence in politics, academia, think tanks, journalism, public relations, business, and culture, as current law requires.
- Strengthen the 1930s law governing foreign agents in the United States, to impose stiffer penalties, including imprisonment.
- Require the FBI and CIA to issue joint annual reports, both classified and unclassified, on the nature and extent of Russian propaganda and information war against the United States and its interests.
- Prioritize intelligence collection and competent analysis of corruption, criminal action, and other behavior that Russian society finds intolerable, to have as a deterrent to, and retaliation against, Kremlin propaganda and information war.
- Strengthen the abilities of friendly countries to retaliate in-kind, especially where U.S. law or procurement procedures limit or handicap such capabilities.

CONCLUSION

Moscow's strength in waging international information war has less to do with its own unique capabilities, and more with the West's learned helplessness to innovate new ways to prevent, deter, or retaliate. The Kremlin has modernized Soviet methods with mainly American communications technologies and channels to create a nimble, entertaining, interesting, and frustratingly persistent fire hose of falsehood designed to undermine, divide, and demoralize its Western targets. Russia's information war easily exploits gaps in U.S. and allied worldview and messaging doctrine. For all the domestic demographic, economic, industrial, territorial, and other problems Putin faces, the Russian leader has freed the Kremlin from its Cold War-era bureaucratic and legalistic inefficiency and slowness. The West has not done the same for itself.

Black Sea Energy Deposits As a Prime Factor in Russia's Annexationof Crimea and its Current Militarization*

By Roger W. Robinson, Jr.

Since the invasion and annexation of Crimea, Russia has offered a number of explanations to justify its actions, including the seizing militarily of Ukrainian territory. The most prominent of these fatuous justifications is that Moscow was protecting ethnic Russians who wished to join the Russian Federation. Upon closer scrutiny, however, a more sinister economic and financial (E&F) narrative is revealed. At the outset, we should note that we have consistently viewed strategic E&F designs heading the list of explanations for the initial annexation as well as the most recent surge in military activity in Crimea and the Black Sea (since end-July 2016). This E&F narrative is offered below.

OIL AND GAS DISCOVERIES IN THE BLACK SEA

In the run up to hostilities in eastern Ukraine that began in early 2014, there had been a number of significant oil and gas discoveries across the Black Sea. Western oil majors discovered some two years before the Kremlin's military incursion into Ukraine that the waters within its Exclusive Economic Zone (EEZ) off Crimea held some of the richest oil and gas reserves in the region, while the fields within Russia's EEZ appeared considerably less promising.

Had Ukraine been given time to fully exploit their offshore reserves, it could not only have ended its energy dependency on Russia, but made the country a net energy exporter. This development would have delivered a major blow to Putin's

---

* This article originally was issued as a report by Roger Robinson for his international consulting firm, RWR Advisory Group, on September 26, 2016.

strategic/political agenda in his "near abroad." Russia's political influence in the region would also surely have been set-back, the centerpiece of which is to return Russia to its former geopolitical stature, lost with the collapse of the Soviet Union. By seizing these Ukrainian assets, Russia has helped assure its sway, and in some cases dominance, with regard to European energy markets.

THE SEIZING OF CRIMEA'S OFFSHORE ASSETS

After the annexation of Crimea, Russia moved quickly to secure all relevant, Ukrainian energy equipment and infrastructure. The primary Ukrainian energy company operating in Crimea (Chornomornaftogaz) was quickly nationalized, and Russia began to consolidate its control over formerly Ukrainian drill rigs. Over the summer of 2016, Ukrainian forces proved unable to oppose Russian efforts to deploy one of these Ukrainian rigs seized during the annexation within Ukraine's EEZ. Armed Russian vessels escorted the rig as it performed exploratory drilling.[289] Not coincidentally, Russia's updated Sea Doctrine calls for the Federal Security Service (FSB) and the Navy to provide greater protection for its Black Sea assets. Moreover, the Russian Navy has undertaken a number of War Games and exercises in the Black Sea in the period since.

After Romania discovered a deep water gas field in its offshore waters in 2012, President Putin almost immediately, in April 2012, signed an accord with Eni to explore Russia's Black sea shelf. Eni agreed to finance the entire $1 to $1.2 billion of the initial exploration costs and agreed to undertake drilling operations with Rosneft. Oil production from Russia's Black Sea shelf has yet to begin under the Eni/Rosneft partnership. Rosneft also had a deal with ExxonMobil for Black Sea drilling, which was terminated by Western sanctions and cost Exxon over $1 billion in lost revenue.[290]

Prior to the Russian annexation of Crimea and occupation of eastern Ukraine, a number of western energy majors were tasked by Kiev to explore energy deposits in Crimea's offshore waters. ExxonMobil, Royal Dutch Shell and others performed exploratory operations in the Black Sea, the results of which led petroleum analysts to believe it may rival the size of the original deposits found in the North Sea. Accordingly, it is estimated that the value of these resources may exceed $1 trillion. Moreover, a Columbia University Marine geologist, William Ryan, stated that the seized offshore reserves have the highest potential production value of any in the Black Sea. Between 2011 and 2014 (when the annexation took place), Crimean gas production climbed from 1 billion cubic meters (BCM) to 2 BCM in 2014, even prior to serious exploration and development activities.

In May 2012, a presentation by specialists at the European Petroleum Conference publicized studies that judged Ukraine's potential deposits as having "tremendous exploration potential," while Russia's were deemed unattractive. [291] Russia's Lukoil tried to bid on an exploration and extraction deal with Ukraine in August 2012, but was outbid by Exxon and Royal Dutch Shell. The two were ready to spend $735 million to drill a pair of wells off of the southwest coast of Crimea in the Skifska area, which extends to Romania. Analysts continue to assert that the fields with the most potential are all within Crimean waters.[292] According to the Ukrainian government, it would cost as much as $12 billion to develop these reserves. Exxon has suspended its operations since March 2014, while Russia continues to expand its own.[293]

With the annexation of Crimea, Moscow claims – albeit illegally – sovereign rights over an area some 230 miles from the Crimean shoreline. When Russia signed the treaty of annexation with Crimea in March 2014, the document stated that the International Law of the Sea would govern the drawing of boundaries on the Black and Azov seas. Under this law, Russia gained an additional 36,000 square miles to its existing Black Sea holdings. In addition, in the immediate aftermath of the Crimean vote to secede from Ukraine, Crimean officials nationalized Chornomornaftogaz. It was later revealed that Gazprom officials had inquired about gaining control over the Chornomornaftogaz assets in early 2014 – a telling "early warning" indicator to more aggressive action to come.[294, 295]

Accordingly, with the annexation, Russia stole the assets of Chornomornaftogaz, which included 12 drill rigs, the entirety of Crimea's gas infrastructure and nine fields currently being developed. Ukraine's Prosecutor General began litigation on October 10, 2014, against the now Russian-controlled Chornomornaftogaz for the "illegal appropriation" of this property.

In December 2015, Russia seized the Petro Hodovanents and Ukraina drill rigs, both belonging to Chornomornaftogaz[296] and valued at $354 million, from the Odesa gas field. At the time, both were stationed within Ukrainian territorial waters. [297] Russia's FSB and Naval vessels escorted the stolen rigs back to Crimean/Russian territory. Russia called their removal an internal Chornomornaftogaz corporate matter based on an elevated "terrorist threat." The amount of gas extracted from the Odesa natural gas field presently stands at 1.17 BCM per year, which is 50% of the current Crimean annual output.

Russia's New Sea Doctrine – July 2015

In July 2015, Russia adopted a new Sea Doctrine that foreshadowed its plans to exploit further energy resources in the Black Sea. One of the long-term goals outlined in this Doctrine is to "study the geological structure and definition of the resource potential of the continental shelf off the Russian Federation" which would include "government control and regulation of exploration and production" and "development of identified offshore fields and intensive exploration of prospective oil and gas resources on the continental shelf of the Russian Federation."

The Doctrine also ensures,

"The Federal Security Service (FSB) of the Russian Federation organizes and ensures in the framework of its responsibilities the defense and protection of the Federation's state borders, inland waters, territorial sea, exclusive economic zones, continental shelf and their natural resources."[298]

Russia's naval forces are instructed to collaborate with the FSB to this end. Now that Russia considers Crimea its sovereign territory, FSB vessels have already been observed "protecting" drill rigs off the Crimean coast from Ukrainian ships.

Shale Gas Resources in Eastern Ukraine

Ukraine's loss of these potentially vast energy resources is not limited to those off the Crimean coast. In January 2013, the Ukrainian government signed its first shale gas production sharing agreement (PSA) with Shell, a 50-year agreement for the Yuzovska block (located in the Dniepr-Donetsk Basin). Shell withdrew in 2015 in response to Russia's occupation of eastern Ukraine. This region is especially important to Ukraine's energy security as 80% of its proven reserves and 90% of its gas production come from the area. Offshore Crimean reserves, however, were viewed as Ukraine's most prized untapped oil and gas resources and could have allowed the country not only to become energy independent, but, as mentioned earlier, a net exporter.[299]

BOTTOM LINE

Over the past two weeks, Ukraine, as we predicted in a report dated August 8, has initiated new legal action against Russia over lost assets (although the theft of the offshore assets, specifically, we understand, is still outstanding). This fully justified push-back from Kiev, however, will likely not be confined to legal proceedings. The sabotage of drill rigs and other energy development infrastructure, targeted military operations to forestall the extraction of these stolen resources and diplomatic efforts to make Russian-marketed Crimean oil and gas "politically radioactive" commodities in the global energy markets are highly plausible, if not probable.

For its part, Russia will probably welcome any pretext to accelerate its consolidation of these huge offshore assets and further militarize the Black and Azov Seas as well as Crimea (rather than have to invent pretexts as they have done in the past). It is useful to bear in mind that Moscow openly admires China's aggressive island-building/militarization activities in the South China Sea, Beijing's provocations toward Japan in the East China Sea and Turkish President Erdogan's wholesale purges of his opponents facilitated by a failed coup attempt. The Kremlin's attempts to make the Black and Azov Seas, in effect, Russian lakes would help satisfy Putin's craving for recognition internationally and perceived "conquest" at home (hence the deployment of Russia's advanced S-400 air defense system to the Crimean peninsula and other stepped-up military efforts).

In short, the Black Sea region is now in play – and in play militarily and dangerously. The U.S. is sure to be tested and harassed with some regularity as it seeks to maintain freedom of navigation in these seas. Romania is likely an endangered species in the Black Sea as it attempts to extricate itself from Moscow's energy noose and become, itself, a net energy exporter. Ukraine is likely headed for a new echelon of violence, if the predicted escalatory spiral over its Black Sea oil and gas reserves moves into full swing (accompanied by the seeming collapse of the Minsk accord).

The Strange "Death" of Communism

By Cliff Kincaid

The headline, "Did the Soviet Union Really End?" seems like something out of a magazine published by the John Birch Society. But it appeared on August 17, 2016, in the *New York Times*.[300] This op-ed by Masha Green suggested that the fall of the old Soviet Union was a deception, arranged by authorities in Moscow to confuse the West about changes in the Soviet Union and now Russia. The article echoed a defector from the Soviet intelligence service, the KGB, Anatoliy Golitsyn, whose charges were ridiculed decades ago as a fantastic "Monster Plot." Top CIA officials, then and now, thought the Russian communists incapable of planning and carrying out such a plan. [301]

Now, according to the *Washington Post*, U.S. spy agencies "are playing catch-up big time" with Russia, a senior U.S. intelligence official was quoted as saying.[302] The paper said that recent directives from the White House and the Office of the Director of National Intelligence (ODNI) "have moved Russia up the list of intelligence priorities for the first time since the Soviet Union's collapse."

But did the Soviet Union really collapse? And what about those communist regimes which didn't "collapse," such as Communist China and North Korea and Cuba? In addition, there's the South African government, dominated by the South African Communist Party through the African National Congress. In Iran, the regime is run by the "Supreme Leader" Ali Khamenei, a Russian agent "educated" at the KGB's Patrice Lumumba University in Moscow. What's more, literally dozens of communist parties still exist around the world, including perhaps a dozen in the United States, and they hold annual International Meetings of Communist and Workers Parties.

Golitsyn wrote two books, *New Lies For Old* (1984) and *The Perestroika Deception* (1998) trying to alert the American people to the plot. International communism was not dead, he warned. It was changing forms and becoming more sinister in its approach to world domination.

It was Soviet President Mikhail Gorbachev, even while promoting the policy of "perestroika," or the restructuring of the Soviet state, who declared, "In October 1917 we parted with the old world, rejecting it once and for all. We are moving towards a new world, the world of Communism. We shall never turn off that road!"[303]

Robert Buchar wrote the book *And Reality Be Damned... Undoing America: What Media Didn't Tell You about the End of the Cold War and the Fall of Communism in Europe*[304] and produced the documentary "The Collapse of Communism: The Untold Story." Buchar maintains that the Russians have had a long-term strategy of fooling the West and ending the Cold War on Moscow's terms. "The West was unable to develop any counter-strategy because they refused to believe Moscow had this long-range strategy," he says.

A political refugee from former Czechoslovakia, Buchar is not optimistic about the West waking up in time, telling this author in April 2014, "[Russian President Vladimir] Putin will get the Ukraine back and the West is not going to stop it." Indeed, in that same month, General Philip Breedlove, the Supreme Allied Commander of NATO, was warning that the United States under President Obama "was not taking steps it could to help Ukraine better defend itself."[305] Breedlove immediately came under attack by pro-Moscow outlets, including *Russia Today* (RT) television and *The Intercept*, a left-wing website headed by Edward Snowden collaborator Glenn Greenwald.[306] Emails were stolen out of one Breedlove's accounts and he was depicted as stoking tensions with Russia and threatening World War III over Russian aggression in Ukraine.

In its belated recognition that essential facts of life did not change in the transition from the old Soviet Union to Russia, the *New York Times* commented that most of the institutions of the USSR, "along with its memberships in international organizations, passed to a new country called the Russian Federation." Columnist Green noted that these "institutions of a long-running totalitarian regime" had "turned out to be stronger than the men who had set out to reform them." She added, "They resisted change for nearly a decade, and once Vladimir V. Putin became president, they fell into place, easing Russia's regression. Today, life in Russia – where everything is political, where the population is mobilized around leader and nation, where censorship and one-party rule have effectively been restored – is more similar to life in the Soviet Union than at any point in the last 25 years."

In 1991, a giant statue of the founder of the secret police, Felix Dzerzhinsky, had been removed from its pedestal in the center of Moscow. It has since been displayed in a park not far from the Kremlin, was "lovingly restored" this summer, and "There is also talk of putting it back in its old place," Green said.

Analyst Toby Westerman, a contributor to our 2014 book *Back from the Dead: The Return of the Evil Empire*[307] has put together a list of examples [308] of how international communist ideology still guides the conduct of Russian President Putin, a former KGB officer and one-time head of its successor agency, the FSB. "I don't see why it is so difficult to see the ideology behind Putin," Westerman said, noting that Putin has declared, "There is no such thing as a former *Chekist*." (The Cheka was the forerunner to the KGB and stood for the All-Russian Commission for Combating Counter-Revolution and Sabotage.)

As quoted by *Newsweek*,[309] at a meeting with members of the All-Russia People's Front in Stavropol, Russia, on January 25, Putin said, "You know that I, like millions of Soviet citizens, over 20 million, was a member of the Communist Party of the USSR and not only was I a member of the party but I worked for almost 20 years for an organization called the Committee for State Security," referring to the KGB. Putin said, "I was not, as you know, a party member by necessity. I liked Communist and socialist ideas very much and I like them still."

My group, America's Survival, Inc., has assembled over the years various groups of analysts and researchers, and former communist intelligence officials, who have been more accurate about Soviet/Russian intentions than the U.S. intelligence officials we regularly see on national television and quoted in the major newspapers. This is primarily because we have studied communist ideology, especially Marxist dialectics, in order to understand communist techniques of deception. This is an area that goes beyond the usual lavishly financed propaganda and disinformation operations we see in such outlets as RT.

As I recounted in the America's Survival book, *Back from the Dead: The Return of the Evil Empire* a former government official told me what happened when Golitsyn had defected in 1961 and was brought into a room to be debriefed. "He looked around and realized that half the CIA operatives in front of him were KGB double agents whose reports he had read on the other side," this former official told me.

My coauthors and I argue in *Back from the Dead* that while Putin does not use the term "world communism" these days, there can be no doubt, having been trained in Marxism-Leninism by the KGB, he understands where the world is heading and what he is doing. In the America's Survival book *The Sword of Revolution*, we quote a former intelligence community insider who said: "Even though there's no association of Putin to a Communist Party of Russia, the fact that he's President of Russia, certainly suggests that he has the ability to control the movement of almost any political party or political organization and he obviously accepts the Communist Party of Russia." Putin's United Russia party officially runs the regime. The various political parties give the false impression that Russia has functioned as a democratic state.

In 2012, at the "Pumpkin Papers Irregulars" dinner in Washington, D.C., held in honor of ex-communist Whittaker Chambers, the late author and commentator M. Stanton Evans joked about his "Law of Inadequate Paranoia," saying, "No matter how bad you think something is, when you look into it, it is always worse." The comment generated nervous laughter among a crowd of people concerned about America's internal security weaknesses and foreign threats. Evans talked about the problem of "literally hundreds of communists and Soviet agents in the U.S. government" during and after the World War II period that he documents in his book, *Stalin's Secret Agents: The Subversion of Roosevelt's Government,* co-authored with the late Herbert Romerstein.

They document how the Yalta conference, which defined post-World War II Europe and betrayed Eastern European nations to Soviet control, was influenced by the Soviet spy Alger Hiss, the first Acting Secretary-General of the United Nations, a body which today continues to serve as a check on American power by America's enemies and adversaries. Flawed from the start, the world organization has functioned as a communist front and an impediment to freedom and progress in the world. Today, it is also a front for Arab-Muslim interests operating through the Organization of Islamic Cooperation, which wants to outlaw criticism of Islam.

Yalta gave rise to the Soviet empire, the betrayal of Free China, and "half a century of Cold War struggle," Stanton Evans and Herb Romerstein note in their 2013 book *Stalin's Secret Agents: The Subversion of Roosevelt's Government.* The rest is history; millions would die in the Soviet Union, China, Korea, Vietnam, Cambodia and Laos, and Communist regimes would take power in Africa and Latin America. Today, the death toll from communism stands at 100 million.

Michael Ledeen, who worked as a consultant to the National Security Council, Department of State, and Department of Defense during the Reagan administration, when Soviet involvement in global terrorism was highlighted, wrote about the dangers of moles in government affecting policy. In his 2007 book, *The War Against the Terror Masters: Why It Happened. Where We Are Now. How We'll Win,* Ledeen wrote about the discovery of Soviet moles in the CIA, such as Aldrich Ames and Harold Nicholson, and the discovery of one such mole in the FBI, Robert Hanssen. Ledeen writes:

> The discovery that Soviet moles had been at work at the highest levels of the American intelligence community had particular importance in our efforts to combat the terror masters. Agency [CIA] analysts had long insisted that there was no conclusive evidence of Soviet involvement in international terrorism. One now had to wonder if that conclusion had been fed to us through the KGB moles in our midst.

Ledeen wrote about how the intelligence community ignored inside information provided by Soviet defectors, such as the Mitrokhin documents, which exposed the nature of Soviet-backed international terrorism, as well as the identities of "thousands of foreign agents – Western politicians, journalists, movie makers, military officers, and diplomats."

The CPUSA has historically been one of the most loyal, pro-Soviet communist parties in the world and reportedly received substantial financial support from the Soviet Union. Although the CPUSA is not necessarily the preeminent communist organization on the U.S. political scene these days, it still maintains links to the Russian Communist Party and is able to organize and deploy activists in some critical election contests.

Since 1988, the CPUSA has not run its own candidates for president and vice-president, preferring instead to work through the Democratic Party. Its support for Obama in 2008 and 2012 was open and outspoken, with various CPUSA officials, including Jarvis Tyner, openly expressing support for the U.S. President and his agenda. "Better stick with him," Tyner told me in 2010.

America's Survival's 2015 book on Marxist dialectics *The Sword of Revolution and the Communist Apocalypse* documents that there are literally dozens of Marxist and communist groups working in minority communities, on college campuses, and in society at large today. They include:

- Democratic Socialists of America (which backed Obama's political career)
- Communist Party USA
- The Revolutionary Communist Party
- The League of Revolutionaries for a New America
- Socialist Workers Party
- Party for Socialism and Liberation

- Party of Communists, USA
- Labor United in Class Struggle
- U.S. Friends of the Soviet People
- Workers World Party

Some of the most important of these are the Communist Party USA, the Workers World Party (WWP) and the Party for Socialism and Liberation. They collaborate with the Russian, Chinese, North Korean, Cuban, and Iranian governments. In fact, the WWP was investigated by the House Internal Security Committee for its support of the North Korean regime and Arab terrorist groups. But the House Committee was disbanded by liberals in Congress. The WWP organized a 2014 Washington, D.C. pro-Castro event under the watchful eyes of José Ramón Cabañas, Chief of the Cuban Interests Section (and now the Embassy of Cuba). WWP operative Sara Flounders was a speaker at the 2014 "Rhodes Forum," which is sponsored by Vladimir Putin's close associate and former KGB official Vladimir Yakunin. It is also known as the "World Public Forum Dialogue of Civilizations."

Bella Dodd, an organizer for the Communist Party who sat on the CPUSA's National Council, gave a series of lectures in the 1950s, examining communist subversion of society and the Catholic Church in particular. She came back to the church, under the guidance of Bishop Fulton J. Sheen, who "knew that a nominal Christian with a memory of the Cross can be easily twisted to the purposes of evil by men who masquerade as saviors." [310] Her expertise had been in organizing teachers and professors for the communist cause. This is the subject of America's Survival's 2016 book *Marxist Madrassas: The Hostile Takeover of Higher Education in America.* [311]

We have seen a massive security meltdown under Obama. NSA leaker Edward Snowden fled to China and then Russia. His handler, writer Glenn Greenwald, has Marxist and Islamist links. He has, for example, appeared before a Muslim Brotherhood front group, the Council on American-Islamic Relations (CAIR), and a Marxist-Leninist conference co-sponsored by The International Socialist Organization (publisher of *Socialist Worker*). Greenwald proudly accepted "the Izzy Award" in 2014 named in honor of Soviet agent and left-wing journalist I.F. Stone.

On the other hand, anti-communism might be a problem if you want to work for the U.S. Government.

Michael J. Sulick, who worked for the CIA for 28 years, served as chief of CIA counterintelligence from 2002 to 2004, and as director of the National Clandestine Service from 2007 to 2010, insists that "Senator Joseph McCarthy's shrill allegations of pervasive communist infiltration of the US government denigrated scores of civil servants but again surfaced no real spies." Sulick, author of *American Spies: Espionage against the United States from the Cold War to the Present,* says McCarthy was "discredited" and that he ran a "misguided crusade" that "raised American suspicions of government efforts to prevent foreign espionage."

Among his targets, McCarthy, who ran the Senate Permanent Subcommittee on Investigations, investigated *Amerasia,* a pro-Communist magazine, and State Department diplomat John Stewart Service, who was arrested for passing classified information to its editor. Another McCarthy target, Owen Lattimore of the Institute for Pacific Relations, was a communist who was deemed so dangerous that he should be detained in the event of a national emergency.

In fact, the late author M. Stanton Evans produced a "'McCarthyism' by the Numbers" table[312] naming 50 people identified by McCarthy, his aides, or in his committee hearings, and what is now known about them, based on official records. They are Soviet agents, Communists, suspects, or persons who "took the fifth" rather than talk about communist or Soviet activities. Evans also discussed this issue in his 2009 book *Blacklisted by History: The Untold Story of Senator Joe McCarthy and His Fight against America's Enemies.*

The parents of Pulitzer Prize-winning *Washington Post* journalist David Maraniss were among those who pled the Fifth in the 1950s. His parents were both CPUSA members. His status as a red-diaper baby explained why he passed up the opportunity back in 2008 to win another journalism award when he covered up Barack Obama's personal relationship with communist Frank Marshall Davis. Maraniss probably decided it was better for Obama to win the presidency than for the truth to come out.[313]

The CIA, however, is beginning to admit some errors. Former CIA historian Benjamin Fischer wrote in a 2016 article "Double Troubles: The CIA and Double Agents during the Cold War"[314] describing in some detail not only how Soviet-bloc intelligence deceived the West, but how the intelligence community did not inform Congress about the deception. Fischer explains how the KGB fed false data through dozens of double-agents as well as moles in such agencies as the CIA. His article notes: "Intelligence officers have a saying that the only thing worse than knowing there is a mole in your organization is finding the mole."

Fischer helps set the record straight about why massive failures of intelligence or policy occur. Still, as analyst Jeff Nyquist told the author, Fischer "misses the whole game – that the Russians had perfect cover during glasnost and perestroika to run a massive deception operation, namely the 'collapse of communism' deception."

As *the New York Times* column by Masha Green suggests, the "death" of the USSR and the liberalization of Russia have to be understood as designed to allow the KGB operatives running Russia to regroup, and solidify and expand their power. This is basically the view of Anatoliy Golitsyn, the Soviet defector. Considering the nature of the deception and why the U.S. intelligence community was admittedly caught off-guard, it seems now advisable to go back and consider the outlook of James Angleton, former head of the CIA's Counterintelligence Staff, who believed the CIA had been deeply penetrated by Soviet agents and was determined to find the Soviet "moles." He had described Golitsyn, who was born in Ukraine, as "the most valuable defector ever to reach the West."

Robert Buchar interviewed Tennent H. "Pete" Bagley, who became CIA chief of counterintelligence, for his documentary *The Collapse of Communism: The Untold Story*.[315] Bagley, an associate of infamous CIA counterintelligence director James Jesus Angelton, said in the film:

> Golitsyn was certainly telling the truth as he knew it. And there comes the other story. Because Golitsyn had a lot of information about penetrations of Western governments, when that information was passed to the Western governments they became outraged and unhappy because no government wants to discover penetrations in its mist. It's not in the interest of the government, it's not in the interest of the people in power to find out they had been fooled, they had been manipulated and therefore they will take every piece of information they can to reject this.

It is beginning to dawn on some of our military and congressional leaders that we have been fooled, and that our national survival is at stake. The term, "existential threat" is being regularly used by top military officials to describe Putin's Russia.

Before the *New York Times* ran the August 2016 article "Did the Soviet Union Really End," Air Force General Philip M. Breedlove, NATO's supreme allied commander for Europe and commander of U.S. European Command, provided what the Pentagon called a "command update" during a news conference at the Pentagon on June 30, 2016. Breedlove said "for the last 12 to 14 years, we've been looking at Russia as a partner. We've been making decisions about force structure, basing investments, et cetera, et cetera, looking to Russia as a partner."[316] Bluntly speaking, he was saying that the U.S. had been caught unprepared for Russian aggression. Breedlove's remarks constituted an acknowledgement of an intelligence failure.

Breedlove has also described the exodus of refugees from the Middle East as a form of "weaponization" used by Russia and its ally Syria to destabilize Europe,[317] a view that suggests that ISIS is part of a Russian plan.

The scope of the intelligence failure regarding Russia was addressed by the Chairman of the House Intelligence Committee, Rep. Devin Nunes (R-CA), who admitted to CNN's Jake Tapper on April 12, 2016, that the U.S. government had badly "misjudged" the intentions of Putin "for many, many years." He declared, "The biggest intelligence failure that we have had since 9/11 has been the inability to predict the leadership plans and intentions of the Putin regime in Russia." [318]

After the Russian invasion of Georgia in 2008, Rep. Nunes noted, the U.S. continued to engage diplomatically with the Russians, and "we continued to talk to the Russians, and then they invaded Eastern Ukraine."

"We missed that," he said. "And then we completely missed entirely when they put a new base, a new base with aircraft into the Mediterranean, into Syria. We just missed it. We were blind."

During this period of "blindness," the U.S. Congress passed permanent normal trade relations, or PNTR, to expand trade and aid to Russia. PNTR for Russia passed the House by a vote of 365-43 and the Senate by 92-4. The New START treaty, passed by the Senate in response to Obama's demand, has left Russia with a nuclear weapons advantage. Meanwhile, Russia is violating the terms of the 1987 Intermediate-Range Nuclear Forces (INF) Treaty with the United States.

In his 2014 book, *A Very Principled Boy: The Life of Duncan Lee, Red Spy and Cold Warrior*, former CIA officer Mark A. Bradley tells the story of communist Duncan Lee, who infiltrated the CIA's predecessor Office of Strategic Services (OSS) for the Soviets and was never prosecuted or convicted. Communist defector Elizabeth Bentley had exposed Lee, but he continued to deny serving the communists until his death. He was eventually exposed definitively as a Soviet agent by the Venona intercepts of Soviet messages by the NSA. One of the Venona messages named Lee, who worked directly for OSS director Donovan, by the cover name "Koch."

Donovan had called him a "very principled boy" who would not betray his country.

The NSA intercepts were not used at the time to prosecute Lee because of the need to keep the nature and success of the surveillance a secret from the Soviets.

"The sad truth," notes writer Mark LaRochelle, "is that Lee was just one of many identified Soviet agents in the OSS. Others, as we now know from numerous impeccable sources, included Maurice Halperin, Carl Marzani, Franz Neumann, Helen Tenney, Julius and Bella Joseph and Lee's Oxford classmate, Donald Niven Wheeler."[319] In fact, says historian Harvey Klehr, there were at least 16 Soviet agents in the OSS.

McCarthy had been vindicated by the NSA intercepts known as Venona, the code name given to the deciphered Soviet spy communications that had been recorded during and after World War II. They were KGB and GRU messages between Moscow and the Soviet espionage network in the United States.

These included messages related to Soviet espionage efforts against U.S. atomic bomb research involving Julius and Ethel Rosenberg, Americans convicted and executed for passing nuclear weapons secrets to the Soviet Union. The National Cryptologic Museum[320] features an exhibit on Venona, highlighting such traitors as State Department official Alger Hiss, Department of Justice official Judith Coplon, and Department of the Treasury official Harry Dexter White.

Tragically, however, the NSA itself has been infiltrated and compromised. Edward Snowden, now living in Moscow, looks increasingly like the NSA equivalent of Philip Agee, who defected from the CIA and became a Soviet and Cuban agent. Agee died in Havana after writing several books with the help of Cuban intelligence. Snowden, a former consultant to the CIA and NSA, has been charged with espionage.

Agee was on the board of the Organizing Committee for a Fifth Estate, an anti-intelligence group, along with such leftist notables as Marcus Raskin of the Institute for Policy Studies, and Communist ACLU official Frank Donner. The former director of the ACLU's Project on Political Surveillance, Frank Donner was a member of the Communist Party who traveled to Russia and had contacts with Russian espionage agents, according to his FBI file. He wrote several books attacking U.S. intelligence agencies, including the NSA. He especially hated the House Committee on Un-American Activities, which grilled him on his CPUSA activities. He took the Fifth. But Donner had the last laugh, as the committee and its successor, the House Committee on Internal Security, were abolished in the 1970s.

Today, the Congress has no committees, subcommittees, or panels, devoted exclusively to internal security.

"America has really dropped the ball on internal security for the last thirty years," says analyst Trevor Loudon, whose new film, *The Enemies Within* profiles 14 Senators and more than fifty Representatives.[321] "Could your Congressman pass an FBI background check?" is the question posed on the cover of the DVD version of the film. In fact, however, the FBI only provides background information about federal employees, not elected officials.

Former FBI supervisor Max Noel told me that the FBI once utilized a CARL test when it conducted background checks on people for high-level positions. The acronym CARL stands for Character, Associates, Reputation, and Loyalty. No such vetting was done in Obama's case. He could never have passed. Nor could many members of Congress, including some on the intelligence oversight committees.

Loudon is suggesting passage of the Muslim Brotherhood Terrorist Designation Act, to close down the activities of this particular radical Muslim organization and its front groups. He hopes that such legislation could spark creation of new congressional bodies to take internal security seriously again.

It is significant that the Council on American Islamic Relations, a Muslim Brotherhood front, has joined with communists and other radicals who also object to NSA surveillance programs. CAIR was actually part of a press conference on Capitol Hill, where it joined with a "who's who" of the far-left, including Code Pink, the Bradley Manning Support Network, the Institute for Policy Studies, and the American Civil Liberties Union. Manning is a former Army analyst who went on trial for espionage for leaking classified information to WikiLeaks and is now serving 35 years in prison.

There is a reference in former CIA director and Secretary of Defense Leon Panetta's book, *Worthy Fights*, about his meeting with Alexander Vasilyevich Bortnikov, the head of the FSB, which was held in a building that still contained a bust of Lenin. Yet Panetta said he believed that the "superpower conflict of the Cold War" was over. There was another reference in the book to Putin and his "KGB years," having been a Soviet spy, but nothing of substance about his work in East Germany, where he had been based.

A couple of years before then-Secretary of State Hillary Clinton's Russian reset, which failed and backfired, a very important book came out, titled, *Comrade J: The Untold Secrets of Russia's Master Spy in America After the End of the Cold War*, based on interviews with Sergei Tretyakov, the former Russian spymaster based at the U.N. Tretyakov was quoted as saying, "I want to warn Americans...You believe because the Soviet Union no longer exists, Russia now is your friend. It isn't, and I can show you how the SVR (i.e., KGB) is trying to destroy the U.S. even today and even more than the KGB did during the Cold War."

Since intelligence operations continued as if nothing had happened, after the "collapse" of the Soviet Union, why isn't it reasonable to assume that the Russians maintained contacts with international terrorist groups? Perhaps this helps explain why Chairman of the Joint Chiefs of Staff (JCS) Marine Corps General Joseph Dunford made it clear the military would not share intelligence with Russia as part of Obama's new Syria policy. "The U.S. military role will not include intelligence sharing with the Russians," he declared. At the same hearing, conducted by the Senate Armed Services Committee, Dunford labeled Moscow the "most significant challenge" to U.S. national security interests.

His warning was an indication that another "Team B" exercise, once commissioned by the CIA to conduct an alternative assessment of the threats the Soviet Union posed to the security of the United States, has to be unleashed on the intelligence community, in order to determine who blinded us and why. Did "diversity" get in the way of identifying the enemy?

At the same time, the Congress has to take its responsibilities seriously. The liberals will raise a hue and cry, and some conservatives may balk, but it is mandatory and necessary to begin addressing what an old congressional committee used to call "un-American activities" at the highest levels of the U.S. Government.

About the Authors

Stephen Blank is an internationally recognized expert on Russian foreign and defense policies and international relations across the former Soviet Union. He is also a leading expert on European and Asian security, including energy issues. He is a Senior Fellow at the American Foreign Policy Council in Washington. From 1989-2013 he was a Professor of Russian National Security Studies at the Strategic Studies Institute of the U.S. Army War College in Pennsylvania.

Frederick Fleitz is Senior Vice President for Policy and Programs at the Center for Security Policy. He held U.S. government national security positions for 25 years with the CIA, DIA, the Department of State and the House Intelligence Committee staff.

Kevin D. Freeman, CFA, is founder of Freeman Global Holdings, LLC, a specialty consulting firm which shares Freeman's unique understanding of the global capital markets and their intersection with national security issues. He is considered one of the world's leading experts on Economic Warfare and Financial Terrorism, having briefed members of the U.S. House, Senate, present and past CIA, DIA, FBI, SEC, Homeland Security, the Justice Department, as well as local and state law enforcement.

Frank Gaffney is the Founder and President of the Center for Security Policy. Under Gaffney's leadership, the Center has been nationally and internationally recognized as a reputable resource for foreign and defense policy matters. Mr. Gaffney was the Deputy Assistant Security of Defense for Nuclear Forces and Arms Control Policy from 1983 to 1987. Following that he was nominated by President Reagan to become the Assistant Secretary of Defense for International Security Policy.

Dr. Daniel Gouré is Vice President with the Lexington Institute, a nonprofit public-policy research organization headquartered in Arlington, Virginia. He is involved in a wide range of issues as part of the institute's national security program. Dr. Gouré has held senior positions in both the private sector and the U.S. Government, including the Pentagon. He also holds a Masters and Ph.D in Russian studies from Johns Hopkins University.

Cliff Kincaid is President of America's Survival, Inc., a former writer for Ronald Reagan's favorite newspaper, Human Events, and a journalist and media critic. He also serves as Director of the AIM Center for Investigative Journalism.

Roger W. Robinson, Jr, is President and CEO of RWR Advisory Group and former Senior Director of International Affairs at the National Security Council under President Reagan.

David Satter, a senior fellow at the Hudson Institute and a fellow at the Johns Hopkins University School of Advanced International Studies (SAIS), has been writing about Russia and the Soviet Union for four decades.

Dr. Mark B. Schneider is a Senior Analyst with the National Institute for Public Policy. Before his retirement from the Department of Defense Senior Executive Service, Dr. Schneider served in a number of senior positions within the Office of Secretary of Defense for Policy including Principal Director for Forces Policy, Principal Director for Strategic Defense, Space and Verification Policy, Director for Strategic Arms Control Policy and Representative of the Secretary of Defense to the Nuclear Arms Control Implementation Commissions. He also served in the senior Foreign Service as a Member of the State Department Policy Planning Staff.

Dr. J. Michael Waller is a Senior Fellow in Information Warfare at the Center for Security Policy, and a founding editorial board member of NATO's Defense Strategic Communications journal.

Endnotes

1 Allison Quinn, "Vladimir Putin: 'We don't want the USSR back but no one believes us,'" London Telegraph, December 21, 2015.

2 Fionlat Philly, "What's Vladi. Putin Really Wildne, WS, National Interest, February/34 admin.-Putin-http://nationalinterest.org/feature/what-putin-really-wants-12311

3 John McCain, "Obama Has Made America Look Weak," New York Times, March 14, 2014.

4 "Joint Statement from the Department of Homeland Security and Office of the Director of National Intelligence on Election Security," Director of National Intelligence, October 7, 2016. https://www.dni.gov/index.php/newsroom/press-releases/215-press-releases-2016/1423-joint-dhs-odni-election-security-statement

5 Will Dunham, "Kerry condemns Russia's 'incredible act of aggression' in Ukraine," Reuters, March 2, 2014. http://www.reuters.com/article/us-ukraine-crisis-usa-kerry-idUSBREA210DG20140302

6 Stephen Pifer, "George W. Bush Was Tough on Russia? Give Me a Break, Politico, March 24, 2016. http://www.politico.com/magazine/story/2014/03/bush-georgia-obama-ukraine-104929

7 Putin almost certainly considers the Baltic states as falling within Russia's sphere of influence and greatly resents decisions by Latvia, Lithuania and Estonia to join the EU and NATO. There have been growing concerns by Baltic leaders that Russia could attempt incursions into their states similar to its 2014 intervention in Ukraine. These concerns have been amplified by a growing number of naval incidents in the Baltic Sea between Russian and NATO vessels and violations of Baltic airspace by Russian fighters.

8 See David Albright, Andrea Stricker, and Serena Kelleher-Vergantini, "Analysis of the IAEA's Report on the PMD of Iran's Nuclear Program," Institute for Science and International Security, December 8, 2015. http://isis-online.org/isis-reports/detail/analysis-of-the-iaeas-report-on-the-pmd-of-irans-nuclear-program/8

9 For more on the 2015 nuclear deal with Iran, see Fred Fleitz, "Obamabomb: A Dangerous and Growing National Security Fraud," Center for Security Policy, 2016.

10 This was actually not the first example of Syrian chemical weapons use in 2013 – there was credible evidence of this in April 2013 but the Obama administration did not act on this

information until June, when it announced that the United States would provide limited military aid in the form of small arms to the Syrian rebels.

11 Jay Solomon MSNBC interview, August 22, 2016. Available at: http://www.msnbc.com/andrea-mitchell-reports/watch/inside-the-us-iran-struggle-748574275947

12 See Natasha Bertrand and Michael B Kelley, "The startlingly simple reason Obama ignores Syria," Business Insider, June 4, 2015. http://www.businessinsider.com/the-startlingly-simple-reason-obama-ignores-syria-2015-6

13 Jay Solomon and Carol Lee, "Obama Wrote Secret Letter to Iran's Khamenei About Fighting Islamic State," Wall Street Journal, November 6, 2014.

14 "Statement By Senators McCain and Graham on Secretary Kerry's Threat To End Talks With Russia," Press release by Senator John McCain, September 28, 2016. http://www.mccain.senate.gov/public/index.cfm/press-releases?ID=7B58F5CA-72D3-4908-805D-CF09A7245569

15 Angela Dewan, "Vladimir Putin snubs France after Syria war crimes comments," CNN.com, October 11, 2016. http://www.cnn.com/2016/10/11/world/syria-aleppo-conflict/

16 Hilary Clarke and James Masters, "Russian warships sail down British coast, likely en route to Syria." CNN.com, October 21, 2016. http://www.cnn.com/2016/10/20/europe/russia-syria-warships-uk-kuznetsov/index.html

17 Mark Mazetti, Anne Barnard, Eric Schmitt, " Military Success In Syria Is Giving Putin Leverage," New York Times, August 7, 2016.

18 Semih Idiz, "Can Turkey Really Turn to Russia,?" www.al-monitor.com, August 2, 2016.

19 Ece Toksabay and Dmitry Solovyov, "Turkey Proposes Cooperation With Russia In Fighting Islamic State," www.reuters.com, July 5, 2016; "Turkey Ready To Cooperate With Russia In Syria," Gulf News.com, August 11, 2016, www. http://gulfnews.com/news/mena/syria/turkey-ready-to-cooperate-with-russia-in-syria-1.1877742.

20 "Interview With Russian Political Analyst Sergey Karaganov: The Four Reasons Why Russia Intervened in Syria," www.memri.org, Special Dispatch no. 6335, March 2, 2016.

21 Nadezhda K. Arbatova and Alexander A. Dynkin, "World Order After Ukraine," Survival, LVIII, NO. 1, 2016, p. 72.

22 Reid Standish, 'Russia Is Using Syria as a Training Ground for Its Revamped Military and Shiny New Toys," foreignpolicy.com, December 9, 2015; Rowan Scarborough, "Russia Using Syrian Civil War As Testing Ground For New Weapons " Washington Times, February 28, 2016.

23 Steve Lee Myers and Eric Schmitt, "Russia Using Syria as Proving Ground, and the West Takes Notice," New York Times, October 14, 2015, http://www.nytimes.com/2015/10/15/world/middleeast/russian-military-uses-syria-as-proving-ground-and-west-takes-notice.html? _r=0; Dmitry Kornev, "Russian High-Precision Weapons in Syria," Moscow Defense Brief, NO. 3, 2016, pp. 14-16.

24 Ibid.

25 "Russia, Syria Said Using Migrant Crisis As 'Weapon' Against West, Radio Free Europe/Radio Liberty, http://www.rferl.org/articleprintview/27584179.html, March 2, 2016

26 Emre Gurban Akay, "Russia to lift sanctions on Turkey 'gradually': PM," Anadolu Agency, June 30, 2016, http://aa.com.tr/en/economy/russia-to-lift-sanctions-on-turkey-gradually-pm-/600593.

27 Stephen Blank, "No Need to Threaten Us, We Are Frightened of Ourselves: Russia's Blueprint for a Police State," in Stephen J. Blank and Richard Weitz, Eds. The Russian Military Today and Tomorrow: Essays in Memory of Mary Fitzgerald, Carlisle Barracks, PA: Strategic Studies Institute US Army War College, 2010, pp. 19-150; Natsional'naya Strategiya Bezopasnosti Rossii, do 2020 Goda, Moscow, Security Council of the Russian Federation, May 12, 2009, www.scrf.gov.ru, in English (Available from the Open Source Center Foreign Broadcast Information Service, Central Eurasia (Henceforth FBIS SOV), May 15, 2009, in a translation from the Security Council website (Henceforth NSS)

28 Ibid; Blank, pp. 19-150; Andrew Monaghan, Defibrillating the Vertikal? Putin and Russian Grand Strategy, Research Paper, Russia and East European Program, Chatham House, 2014; Andrew Monaghan, Russian State Mobilization: Moving the Country on to a War Footing, Research Paper, Russia and East European Program, Chatham House, 2016 https://www.chathamhouse.org/expert/dr-andrew-monaghan#sthash.ZJ6xK8rL.dpuf

29 Edict of the Russian Federation President, "On the Russian Federation's National Security Strategy," December 31, 2015,

http://www.ieee.es/Galerias/fichero/OtrasPublicaciones/Internacional/2016/Russian-National-Security-Strategy-31Dec2015.pdf

30 "The Foreign Policy Concept of the Russian Federation, 2008, www.fas.org/nuke/guide/russia/doctrine/concept.htm

31 John Loewenhardt, "Russia and Europe: Growing Apart Together," Brown Journal of World Affairs, VII, NO.1, Winter-Spring, 2000, p. 171

32 Ibid.

33 Vitaly Kozyrev, "Russia's Security Policy in Asia in Times of Economic Uncertainty," Paper Presented to the Annual Meeting of the American Political Science Association, September 2-5, 2010, p. 21.

34"Concept of Public Security in the Russian Federation," Moscow, www.kremlin.ru, November 20, 2013, FBIS SOV, January 25, 2014.

35 Ibid

36Michael Weiss, "Russia Is Sending Jihadis to Join ISIS," Daily Beast, August 23, 2015, http://www.thedailybeast.com/articles/2015/08/23/russia-s-playing-a-double-game-with-islamic-terror0.html; International Crisis Group, The North Caucasus Insurgency and Syria: An Exported Jihad? March 16, 2016, pp. 16-17, http://www.crisisgroup.org/en/regions/europe/north-caucasus/238-the-north-caucasus-insurgency-and-syria-an-exported-jihad.aspx.

37 Luke Chambers," Authoritarianism and Foreign Policy: The Twin Pillars of Resurgent Russia," Caucasian Review of International Affairs, IV, NO. 2, 2010, pp. 119-120

38 Ibid., p. 117, Stephen Blank, "The Sacred Monster: Russia as a Foreign Policy Actor," Stephen J. Blank, Ed., Perspectives on Russian Foreign Policy, Carlisle Barracks, PA: Strategic Studies Institute, US Army War College, 2012, pp. 25-194

39 Moscow, Interfax, in English, February 24, 2011, FBIS SOV, February 24, 2011

40 "Medvedev Warns Arabs of 'Extremism,' Al-Jazeera.com, February 22, 2011, http://www.aljazeera.com/news/europe/2011/02/2011222142449923896.html

41 Dmitri Trenin, Russia in the Middle East: Moscow's Objectives, Priorities, and Policy Drivers, Carnegie Moscow Center, April 5, 2015.

42 "Russia's Chechnya, Saudi Arabia Discuss Investments in Region," BBC Monitoring, May 8, 2016; Dmitriy Frolovskiy, "Russia Eyes Mideast Foreign Investment Drive," Trade Arabia, May 22, 2016,

43 Vladislav Inozemtsev, "The Rationale and Goals of Russia's Syria Policy" in "The Kremlin's Actions in Syria: Origins, Timing, and Prospects," Atlantic Council, 2016, pp. 21-25.

44 Ibid., p.22

45 Ibid., pp.22-23

46 Adam Garfinkle, "Russian Motives In Syria and the Implications for U.S. Policy,'" Ibid., pp. 34-35

47 "Syria Asks Russia To Rebuild its Oil Industry," Press TV.com, May 20, 2016, http://www.presstv.ir/Detail/2016/05/20/466598/Syria-asks-Russia-to-rebuild-its-oil-industry.

48 Dmitri Trenin, "All Change in the Russian-Western Strategic Climate," Carnegie Europe report, February 14, 2016, http://carnegieeurope.eu/strategiceurope/?fa=62767.

49 Stephen Blank, Shrinking Ground: Russia's Decline in Global Arms Sales, Occasional Paper, Jamestown Foundation, Washington, D.C. October, 2010

50 John W. Parker, "Understanding Putin Through a Middle Eastern Looking Glass," Institute for National Strategic Studies, National Defense University, Fort Leslie McNair, Washington, D.C, 2015, pp. 25-39

51 Andrew E. Kramer, "Unrest in Libya and the Middle East Is Costing the Russian Arms Industry," New York Times, March 4, 2011

52 William Burns cable leaked by Wikileaks, "Addressing Russian Arms Sales," October 26, 2007. Available at https://wikileaks.org/plusd/cables/07MOSCOW5154_a.html (Henceforth Burns)

53 Ibid.

54 Alexey Malashenko, Russia and the Muslim World, Carnegie Moscow Center, Working Papers, No. 3, 2008, p. 8

55 Roland Dannreuther, "Russia and the Middle East: a Cold War Paradigm,?" Europe-Asia Studies LXIV, NO. 3, 2012, p.558

56 Quoted in Gordon G. Chang, "How China and Russia Threaten the World," Commentary, June 2007, p. 29

57 Thomas Ambrosio, "Russia's Quest for Multipolarity: A Response to US Foreign Policy in the Post-Cold War Eta," European Security XIX, NO. 1, Spring, 2006, p. 54

58 Ibid., p. 59

59 Alvin Z. Rubinstein, "Moscow and Tehran: The Wary Accommodation" in Alvin Z.
Rubinstein and Oles M. Smolansky, Eds., Regional Power Rivalries in the New Eurasia:
Russia, Turkey, and Iran, New York: Taylor and Francis, 2016. pp.31-32

60 Moscow, Komsomolskaya Pravda, in Russian, March 21, 1996, FBIS-SOV-96-056, March
21, 1996, p. 16, The Jamestown Monitor, March 14, 1996

61 Tehran, Irna, in English, March 8, 1995, FBIS-NES-95-045, March 8, 1995, p. 51.

62 Tehran, Abrar in Persian, March 7, 1995, FBIS-NES-95-052, March 17, 1995, pp. 71-72,
Paris AFP, in English, March 21, 1995, FBIS-NES-95-056, March 23, 1995, pp. 47-48,
Judith Perera, "Russia: Stepping Into the Gulf", Middle East International, March 20,
1995, p. 13, Moscow, Interfax, in English, December 5, 1995, FBIS-SOV-95-234,
December 6, 1995, p. 25, Stephen Grummon, Introduction, "Russian Ambitions in the
Persian Gulf" Middle East Quarterly, II, No. 1, March, 1995, pp. 87-92, Alexei Vassiliev,
Russian Foreign Policy in the Middle East: From Messianism to Pragmatism, Reading:
Ithaca Press, 1993, p. 360.

63 Tehran, IRNA in English, May 30, 1995, FBIS-NES-95-104, May 31, 1995, pp. 65-66.

64 Tehran, IRNA, in English, July 20, 1998, FBIS-NES-98-201, July 21, 1998.

65 Emil Aslan Suleimanov, "Mission Accomplished? Russia's Withdrawal From Syria, Middle
East Policy, 2016,p.2

66 Zen Adra, "Putin to Assad: We Won't Let You Lose,"Al-Masdar News, April 19, 2016
https://www.almasdarnews.com/article/putin-assad-wont-let-lose/ | Al-Masdar News

67 "Report: Vladimir Putin Asked Bashar Al-Assad to Resign," Time, January 22, 2016,
http://time.com/4189997/report-putin-asked-bashar-al-assad-to-resign/

68 "Russia: 95,000 Russian troops in largest military exercise, Deutsche Welle, September 14,
2015, http://www.dw.com/en/95000-russian-troops-in-largest-military-exercise/a-
18713214

69 "No Permanent Strategic Bombers & Nukes in Syria But Khmeimim Base To Be Enlarged –
Russian Senator," RT, August 11, 2016. https://www.rt.com/news/355516-khmeimim-
base-russia-enlargement/

70 Stephen Blank, "The Black Sea and Beyond: Naval and Strategic Consequences of Russia's
Invasion of Ukraine," Forthcoming, Proceedings of the U.S. Naval Institute; Moscow,
Interfax, in English, July 27, 2014, FBIS SOV, July 27, 2014

71 Bruce Jones. "Russia searches for strategic airbase partner" IHS Jane's Defense Weekly. March 4, 2014 http://www.janes.com/article/34916/russia-searches-for-strategic-airbase-partners.

72 Ibid.

73 Ivan Nechepurenko, "Russia Seeks to Reopen Military Bases in Vietnam and Cuba," New York times, Ocotber 7, 2016, www.nytimes.com

74 "Russian Defense Minister Vows to Strengthen Navy," Agence France Presse, August 19, 2014,

75 Moscow, Interfax, in English, June 20, 2014, FBIS SOV, June 20, 2014

76 Moscow, Interfax, in English, May 20, 2014, FBIS SOV, May 20, 2014; Stephen Blank, "Russian Strategy and Policy in the Middle East," Israel Journal of Foreign Relations, VIII, NO. 2, May 2014, pp. 9-25.

77 Captain Thomas S. Fedyszyn, USN, "The Russian Navy 'Rebalances' to the Mediterranean," Proceedings of the US Naval Institute, December 2013.

78 Stephen Blank, "The Black Sea and Beyond," Proceedings of the US Naval Institute, October, 2015, pp. 36-41.

79 Stephen Blank, "The Meaning of Russia's Naval Deployments in the Mediterranean," Eurasia Daily Monitor, March 4, 2016

80 Bassem Mroue, "Russia Builds Military camp Near Ancient Site In Palmyra," Associated Press, May 17, 2016, http://www.cbs46.com/story/31990649/russians-building-army-base-at-syrias-palmyra-site.

81 Sergei Lavrov, "Vneshnepoliticheskaya Samostoyatel'nost' Rossii Bezuslovnyi Imperativ," (Russia's Foreign Policy Autonomy is an Unconditional Imperative) Moskovskiye Novosti, January 19, 2007, http://www.mn.ru/issue.php?2007-1-56.

82 Samia Nakhoul, "Syria's Assad Shows No Willingness To Compromise," Reuters, April 8, 2016, http://www.reuters.com/article/us-mideast-crisis-syria-insight-idUSKCN0X50O0

83 Toksabay and Solovyov; op. cit.: "Turkey Ready To Cooperate With Russia In Syria;" Akay, op. cit.; Idiz, op. cit.

84 Trenin, op. cit.

85 "Russia to reach New START ceilings by 2028 (Part 2)," Interfax-AVN, January 14, 2011, available at http:// business.highbeam.com/407705/article-1G1-246550534/russia-reach-new-start-ceilings-2028.

86 National Intelligence Council, "Global Trends 2030: Alternative Worlds," National Intelligence Council, December 2012, p. 69, available at http://www.dni.gov/nic/globaltrends.

87 Keith B. Payne and John S. Foster, et. al., Russian Strategy: Expansion, Crisis and Conflict (Fairfax, VA: National Institute Press, 2016), pp. xi, available at http://www.nipp.org/wp-content/uploads/2016/01/FINAL-FOR-WEB-1.12.16.pdf.

88 Robin Emmott, "Risk of nuclear war in Europe growing, warns Russian ex-minister," Reuters, March 19, 2016, available at http://www.reuters.com/article/us-ukraine-crisis-russia-idUSKCN0WL0EV.

89 Payne and Foster, et. al., Russian Strategy: Expansion, Crisis and Conflict, op. cit., p. 1.

90 Matthew Rosenberg, "Joint Chiefs Nominee Warns of Threat of Russian Aggression," The New York Times, July 9, 2015, available at http://www.nytimes.com/2015/07/10/us/general-joseph-dunford-joint-chiefs-confirmation-hearing.html?_r=0).: Morgan Chalfant, "Top Pentagon Generals Deem Russia Largest 'Existential Threat' to U.S.," The Washington Free Beacon, July 15, 2015, available at http://freebeacon.com/national-security/top-pentagon-generals-deem-russia-largest-existential-threat-to-u-s/.

91 Mark B. Schneider, "Nuclear Deterrence in the Context of the European Security Crisis and Beyond," The Heritage Foundation, December 21, 2015, pp. 3-4, available at http://www.heritage.org/research/reports/2015/12/nuclear-deterrence-in-the-context-of-the-european-security-crisis-and-beyond.

92 Pavel Felgenhauer, "Western Policy Toward Russia: Swinging Between Deterrence and Appeasement," Eurasia Daily Monitor, Volume 13 Issue 98, May 19, 2016 available at http://www.jamestown.org/single/?tx_ttnews%5Btt_news%5D=45448&no_cache=1#.V2FS3a JOyUk.

93 Ibid.

94 "The dangers of our aging nuclear arsenal," The Week.com, January 17, 2015, available at http://theweek.com/ articles/533721/dangers-ouraging-nuclear-arsenal.

95 Mark B. Schneider, "The Triad's Uncertain Future," The Journal of International Security Affairs, No. 23 (Fall Winter 2012), pp. 21-28, available at http://www.securityaffairs.org/sites/default/files/issues/archives/FW2012 covertocover.pdf.

96 Mark B. Schneider, "The Nuclear Doctrine and Forces of the Russian Federation," (Fairfax Va.: National Institute for Public Policy, 2006), pp. 19-26, available at http://nipp.org/Publication/downloads/Publication%20Archive% 20PDF/Russian%20nuclear %20doctrine%20--%20NSF%20 for%20print.pdf.

97 "Russia to broaden nuclear strike options," RT, October 14, 2009, available at http://rt.com/news/russia-broaden-nuclear-strike/.: "Russia's New Military Doctrine Does Not Rule Out Possible Nuclear Strike – Patrushev," Daily News Bulletin, November 20, 2009, available at http://search.proquest.com/professional/login.

98 "Russia may face large-scale military attack, says Strategic Missile Troops chief," BBC Monitoring Former Soviet Union, December 16, 2009, available at http://search.proquest.com/professional/login.

99 "Russia will use nukes in case of a strike – official," RT, December 12, 2013, available at http://rt.com/politics/ nuclear-strike-attack-rogozin-053/.

100 "Russia classifies information on pre-emptive nuclear strikes – military," BBC Monitoring Former Soviet Union, September 5, 2014, available at http://search.proquest.com/professional/login.

101 Ilya Kramnik, "Cold-Calculation Apocalypse. NATO Has Taken Notice of the Russian Nuclear Threat," Lenta.ru, February 3, 2015, available at http://lenta.ru/articles/2015/02/03/apocalipsis/. (In Russian).

102 Vladimir Sokirko, "Top-ol, Top-ol!!" Moskovskiy Komsomolets, December 23, 1999.: Simon Saradzhyan, Russia's Non-strategic Nuclear Weapons in Their Current Configuration and Posture: A Strategic Asset or Liability?, (Harvard Belfer Center, January 2010), p. 18, available at http://belfercenter.ksg.harvard.edu/files/russian-position-NSNWs .pdf.

103 Payne and Foster, et. al., Russian Strategy: Expansion, Crisis and Conflict, op. cit., pp. 46, 48-50, 52, 62, 69-71, 109, 111.

104 Jens Stoltenberg, The Secretary General's Annual Report 2015, (Brussels: The North Atlantic Treaty Organization, January 2016), p. 19, available at http://www.nato.int/nato_static_fl2014/assets/pdf/pdf_2016_01/20160128_SG _AnnualReport_2015_en.pdf.

105 David A. Shlapak and Michael W. Johnson, Reinforcing Deterrence on NATO's Eastern Flank (Washington, D.C.: RAND Corporation, 2016) p. 4, available at

http://www.rand.org/content/dam/rand/pubs/research_reports/
RR1200/RR1253/RAND_RR1253.pdf.

106 Will Stewart, "Moscow Troops Could Be in Five NATO Capitals in Two Days, Boasts
Putin: Leader Boasted to Ukrainian President About Russian Power," The Daily Mail,
September 18, 2014, available at http://www.dailymail. co.uk/news/article-
2761195/Moscow-troops-five-NATO-capitals-two-days-boasts-Putin-Leader-boasted-
Ukrainian-president-Russian-power.html.

107 "Direct Line with Vladimir Putin," The Kremlin, April 17, 2014, available at
http://eng.kremlin.ru/news/7034.

108 Sir Adrian Bradshaw, "The latest security challenges facing NATO," Rusi, February 20,
2015, available at https://
www.rusi.org/go.php?structureID=videos&ref=V54E7621089708#.VTFlcJN4d0T.

109 Dr. Jacob W. Kipp, "Russia's Nonstrategic Nuclear Weapons." Military Review, May-June
2001, available at http:
//fmso.leavenworth.army.mil/documents/russias_nukes/russias_nukes.htm.

110 Robert Work and James Winnefeld, "Statement Of Robert Work, Deputy Secretary Of
Defense, and Admiral James Winnefeld, Vice Chairman Of The Joint Chiefs of Staff,
before the House Committee on Armed Services June 25, 2015," p. 4, available at
http://docs.house.gov/meetings/AS/AS00/20150625/ 103669/HHRG-114-AS00-Wstate-
Workr-20150625.pdf.

111 "Statement of Robert Scher Assistant Secretary of Defense for Strategy, Plans, and
Capabilities before the House Armed Services Subcommittee on Strategic Forces March
2, 2016," p. 3, available at
http://docs.house.gov/meetings/AS/AS29/20160302/104619/HHRG-114-AS29-Wstate-
ScherR-20160302.pdf.

112 "Testimony Prepared By: Dr. Keith B. Payne Professor and Head, Graduate Department of
Defense and Strategic Studies Missouri State University Commissioner, Congressional
Strategic Posture Commission," before the United States Senate Appropriations
Subcommittee on Energy and Water Development July 25, 2012, available at http://
www.google.com/url?sa=t&rct=j&q=&esrc=s&source=web&cd=1&ved=0CC4QFj
AA&url=http%3A%2F%2Fwww. approcould-become-nuclear-
targets.html.priations.senate.gov%2Fht-energy.cfm%3Fmethod%3Dhearings.

113 "Putin threatens to retarget missiles," UPI, February 14, 2008, available at http://www.upi.com/Top_News/ 2008/02/15/Putin-threatens-to-retarget-missiles/UPI-76031203057018/.

114 "Russia: We may use nukes if threatened," The Jerusalem Post, January 19, 2008, available at http://www.Jpost .com/International/Russia-We-may-use-nukes-if-threatened.

115 "Russia could target missiles at sites in Central Europe," Sputnik News, September 10, 2015, available at http:// sputniknews.com/russia/20080910/116678626.html.

116 "Russia's New Military Doctrine Does Not Rule Out Possible Nuclear Strike – Patrushev," Russia's New Military Doctrine Does Not Rule Out Possible Nuclear Strike – Patrushev," Daily News Bulletin, November 20, 2009, available at http://search.proquest.com/professional/login.

117 Julian Isherwood, "Russia warns Denmark its warships could become nuclear targets," Telegraph.com, March 21, 2015, available at http://www.telegraph.co.uk/news/worldnews/europe/denmark/11487509/Russia-warns-Denmark-its-warships-.

118 Andrew E. Kramer, "Russia Calls New U.S. Missile Defense System a 'Direct Threat,'" The New York Times, May 12, 2016, available at http://www.nytimes.com/2016/05/13/world/europe/russia-nato-us-romania-missile-defense.html.: Fox News and the Associated Press, "Putin Warns Romania, Poland over Implementing US Missile Shield," Fox News, May 28, 2016, available at http://www.foxnews.com/world/2016/05/28/putin-warns-romania-poland-over-implementing-us-missile-shield.html?intcmp =hpbt1.

119 Keith B. Payne, "Putin Wields the Nuclear Threat —and Plays with Fire," National Review Online, June 30, 2015, http://www.nationalreview.com/article/420510/russias-nuclear-strategy-coercion-and-intimidation.: National Institute for Public Policy, Russia's Nuclear Posture, (Fairfax, VA: National Institute Press, 2015), available at http://www.nipp.org/wp-content/uploads/2015/04/Russias-Nuclear-Posture .pdf.; Zachary Keck, "Russia Threatens Nuclear Strikes Over Crimea," The Diplomat, July 11, 2014, available at http://thediplomat.com/2014/ 07/russia-threatens-nuclear-strikes-over-crimea/.

120 "U.S. Presence In Eastern Europe Is Vital, Commanding General Says," National Public Radio, February 5, 2016, available at http://www.npr.org/2016/02/05/465672051/u-s-presence-in-eastern-europe-is-vital-commanding-general-says.

121 "2016 Deterrence Symposium Gen. Curtis M. Scaparrotti La Vista Conference Center, La Vista, NE," July 27, 2016, available at http://www.stratcom.mil/speeches/2016/178/2016_Deterrence_Symposium/.

122 Alexander Golts, "Russia Has Dangerously Altered the Status Quo," The Moscow Times, September 8, 2014, available at http://www.themoscowtimes.com/opinion/article/russia-has-dangerously-altered-the-status-quo/ 506632.html.

123 "NATO's Nuclear Forces in the New Security Environment," (Brussels: NATO, October 2009), pp. 1, 3, available at http://www.nato.int/nato_static/assets/pdf/pdf_topics/20091022_Nuclear_Forces_in_the_ew_Security_Environment-eng.pdf.

124 "Evidence of Russian Development of New Sub-Kiloton Nuclear Warheads," Office of Transnational Issues, Central Intelligence Agency," August 30, 2000, pp. 1, 10, available at http://www.gwu.edu/~nsarchiv/NSAEBB/ NSAEBB200/index.htm_.

125 William J. Perry and James R. Schlesinger, America's Strategic Posture - The Final Report of the Congressional Commission on the Strategic Posture of the United States, (Washington D.C.: U.S. Institute of Peace, 2009), p. 12, available at http://media.usip.org/reports/strat_posture_report.pdf.

126 "Russian forces practice rocket fire," Interfax, May 8, 2014, available at http://dialog.proquest.com/
professional/login.: Bill Gertz, "Russia Conducts Large-Scale Nuclear Attack Exercise," The Washington Free Beacon, May 8, 2014, available at http://freebeacon.com/national-security/russia-conducts-large-scale-nuclear-attack-exercise/.

127 Adrian Croft, "Russia's nuclear strategy raises concerns in NATO," Reuters, February 4, 2015, available at http: //www.reuters.com/article/2015/02/04/us-ukraine-crisis-russia-nuclear-insight.

128 Mark B. Schneider, "Nuclear Deterrence in the Context of the European Security Crisis and Beyond," The Heritage Foundation, December 21, 2015, p. 6, available at http://www.heritage.org/research/reports/2015/ 12/nuclear-deterrence-in-the-context-of-

the-european-security-crisis-and-beyond.; Piotr Butowski, "Russia's Air Force 2025," Air International, January 2014, pp. 98-99.

129 U.S. Department of Energy and U.S. Department of Defense, National Security and Nuclear Weapons in the 21st Century, September 2008, p. 8, available at http://www.aps.org/policy/reports/popareports/upload/nuclear-weapons.pdf.: "Military Dominance over Russia Impossible, Nuclear Deterrent Top Priority – Defense Ministry," RT, January 30, 2015, available at http://rt.com/news/227811-russia-military-supremacy-modernization.; "New Heavy ICBM to Be Put Into Service in 2018—Karakayev," Sputnik News, May 5, 2011, available at http://sputniknews.

com/voiceofrussia/2012_12_14/Russia-to-build-new-heavy-ICBM-by-2018-Karakayev/.; Steve Gutterman, "Russia Plans New ICBM to Replace Cold War 'Satan' Missile," Reuters, December 17, 2013, available at http://www. reuters.com article/2013/12/17/us-russia-missiles-idUSBRE9B G0SH20131217.; "Russia to Revive Nuclear Missile Trains— RVSN Commander," Interfax, December 16, 2014, available at http://search. proquest.com/ Professional/login.; "Deployment of First Regiment With New Strategic Missile Complex Will Begin in 2014 -- General Staff," Interfax-AVN, June 7, 2013 (Transcribed by World News Connection).; Mark B. Schneider, "Russia's Noncompliance with Arms Control Obligations," Gatestone Institute, July 31, 2013, available at http://www. gatestoneinstitute.org/3906/russia-arms-control.; National Air and Space Intelligence Center, Ballistic and Cruise Missile Threat, 2013, available at http://www.afisr.af.mil/shared/ media/.; Vitaliy Ankov, "Russian 5G Subs to Be Equipped with Ballistic, Cruise missiles—Source," RIA Novosti, March 19, 2011,available at http://en.ria.ru/military _news/20110319/163091053.htm.; "Russia Goes Ahead with 5G Submarine Project," Ria Novosti, March 8, 2013, available at http://en.rian.ru/military_news/20130318/180092 698/Russia-Goes-Ahead-with-5G-Submarine-Project.htm.; "Russia Speeds Up Development of New Strategic Bomber," RIA Novosti, November 28, 2013, available at http://en.ria.ru/military_news/20131128/ 185110769/Russia-Speeds-Up-Development-of-New-Strategic-Bomber.html.; "Russia's New Bomber to Carry Hypersonic Weapons – Source," Sputnik News, August 30, 2013, available at http://sputniknews.com/military/20130830/183062128/Russias-New-Bomber-to-Carry-Hypersonic-Weapons--Source.html.; "Meeting with Members of Political Parties Represented in the State Duma," The Kremlin, August 14, 2014, available at http://eng.kremlin.ru/transcripts/228205.;"Russia to Produce Successor of Tu-160 Strategic Bomber After 2023," Sputnik News, June 4, 2015, available at http://sputniknews.com/ military/20150604/1022954769.html.; "The Kremlin, Meeting with Members of Political Parties Represented in the State Duma," August 14, 2014, available at http://eng.kremlin.ru/transcripts/22820.; "Russia to Produce Successor of Tu-160 Strategic Bomber After 2023," Sputnik News, June 4, 2015, available at http://sputniknews.com/military/ 20150604/1022954769.html.; "Russia Developing Two Types of Advanced Liquid-Fuel ICBMs," Interfax, August 25, 2012, available at http://search. proquest.com/professional/login.; Lynn Berry and Vladimir Isachenkov, "Kremlin-controlled TV airs 'secret' plans for nuclear weapon," Associated Press, November 12, 2015, available at http:// bigstory.ap.org/articleaaa 75e4bb6e84d 52948b9e6 d8275c71d/kremlin-controlled-tv-airs-secret-plans-nuclear-weapon.; "Text of Russian TV reports featuring classified weapon system Status-6," BBC Monitoring Former Soviet Union, November 2015, available at http:/search.proquest.com/Professional/login.; Bill Gertz, "CIA: Leak of Nuclear-Armed Drone Sub Was Intentional," The Washington Free Beacon, November 19, 2015, available at http: //free beacon.com/national-security/cia-leak-of-nuclear-armed-drone-sub-was-intentional/.; "Russia to Test Upgraded Yars Ballistic Missile in Next Few Months," Sputnik News, May 16, 2015, available at http://sputniknews com/russia/20160516/10396 98974/russia-yars-missile-test.html.; "Russia's Dmitry Donskoy sub to participate in testing of upgraded Bulava missile — source," TASS, June 21, 2016, available at http: //tass.ru/en/defense/883679.

130 "Moscow Emphasizes Quality of its Nuclear Potential," Ghana.mid.ru, January 13, 2005, available at http://www. ghana.mid.ru/ nfr/nfr331.html_.

131 "Nuclear Munitions to be Improved and Revitalized --Russian Federation Ministry of Defense," Ria Novosti, September 4, 2009. (Translated by World News Connection.)

132 Central Intelligence Agency, "Evidence of Russian Development of New Subkiloton Nuclear Warheads [Redacted]," Intelligence Memorandum, August 30, 2000, approved for release October 2005, p. 6, available at http://www.foia.cia.gov/sites/default/files/document_conversions/89801/DOC_00012604 63.pdf.: Robert R. Monroe, "A Perfect Storm over Nuclear Weapons," Air and Space Journal, Vol. 23, No. 3 (Fall 2009), available at

http://www.airpower.au.af.mil/airchronicles/apj/apj09/fal09/monroe.html.; Mark B. Schneider, The Nuclear Forces and Doctrine of the Russian Federation, (Fairfax Va.: National Institute Press, 2006), pp. 15-16, available at http://www.nipp.org/wp-content/uploads/2014/12/Russian-nuclear-doctrine-NSF-for-print.pdf.

133 "Russian Pundit Litovkin Argues Case of Bulava," Ekho Moskvy, July 20, 2009, available at http://search.Proquest .com/professional/login.: Andrei Kislyakov, "Does Russia Need a 'Half-Baked' Missile and Another New Tank?," Sputnik News, January 1, 2008, available at http.www//sputniknews.com/analysis/20080115/9672 8277.html.; Ilya Kramnik, "Nevsky and Novomoskovsk: Two submarines for Putin," Ria Novosti, December 15, 2010, available at http://www.freerepublic.com/focus/f-news/2642985/posts.

134 "Commander notes current, future Russian ICBMs' potential against missile defence," BCC Monitoring of Former Soviet Union, December 18, 2011, available at http://english.cri.cn/6966/2011/12/16/ 2021s671932.htm.: "Russia tests hypersonic warheads for its newest ICBMs – paper," BBC Monitoring Former Soviet Union, May 7, 2016, available at http://dialog.proquest.com/professional/login; "Russia to Develop Precision Conventional ICBM Option," Cihan News Agency, December 14, 2012, available at http://dialog.proquest.com/professional/login.: "Sarmat ICBM serial production to begin in 2018-2019 - deputy defense minister (Part 2)," Interfax, April 20, 2015, available at http://dialog.proquest.com/professional/login.

135 "Obama Advisor Gary Samore, 'The Ball is Very Much in Tehran's Court," Radio Free Europe, April 14, 2011, available at http://www.rferl.org/content/interview samore_russia_iran_us_policy/3557326.html.

136 "James N. Miller, Principal Deputy Under Secretary of Defense for Policy, Statement before the House Commit-tee on Armed Services, November 2, 2011," available at http://armedservices.house.gov/index.cfm/files/serve? File_id=faad05df-9016-42c5-86bc-b83144c635c9.

137 "New RF-US agreement to replace START to be concluded before year end – FM," ITAR-TASS, March 9, 2009, available at http://www.itar-tass.com/eng/level2.html?NewsID=14295189& PageNum=1.

138 Aleksey Arbatov, "Tactical Nuclear Weapons: Problems and Solutions: Strategic Offensive Weapon Reductions Could Extend to Nonstrategic Munitions," Voyenno-

Promyshlenny Nezavisimoye Online, May 20, 2011, available at http://www.dialog.com/proquestdialog/.: Aleksey Arbatov, "'Concepts': Nonstrategic Nuclear Weapons; Dilemmas and Approaches; The Path to a Nuclear-Free World Promises To Be Long," Moscow Nezavisimoye Voyennoye Obozreniye Online, May 20, 2011. (Translated by World News Connection).; "In a Broad Context," Krasnaya Zvezda Online, April 29, 2011. (Translated by World News Connection).

139 Schneider, The Nuclear Forces and Doctrine of the Russian Federation, op. cit., pp. 139 "Russian Pundit Litovkin Argues Case of Bulava," Ekho Moskvy, July 20, 2009, available at http://search.Proquest .com/professional/login.: Andrei Kislyakov, "Does Russia Need a 'Half-Baked' Missile and Another New Tank?," Sputnik News, January 1, 2008, available at http.www//sputniknews.com/analysis/20080115/9672 8277.html.; Ilya Kramnik, "Nevsky and Novomoskovsk: Two submarines for Putin," Ria Novosti, December 15, 2010, available at http://www.freerepublic.com/focus/f-news/2642985/posts.

139 "Commander notes current, future Russian ICBMs' potential against missile defence," BCC Monitoring of Former Soviet Union, December 18, 2011, available at http://english.cri.cn/6966/2011/12/16/ 2021s671932.htm.: "Russia tests hypersonic warheads for its newest ICBMs – paper," BBC Monitoring Former Soviet Union, May 7, 2016, available at http://dialog.proquest.com/professional/login; "Russia to Develop Precision Conventional ICBM Option," Cihan News Agency, December 14, 2012, available at http://dialog.proquest.com/professional/login.: "Sarmat ICBM serial production to begin in 2018-2019 - deputy defense minister (Part 2)," Interfax, April 20, 2015, available at http://dialog.proquest.com/professional/login.

139 "Obama Advisor Gary Samore, 'The Ball is Very Much in Tehran's Court," Radio Free Europe, April 14, 2011, available at http://www.rferl.org/content/interview samore_russia_iran_us_policy/3557326.html.

139 "James N. Miller, Principal Deputy Under Secretary of Defense for Policy, Statement before the House Commit-tee on Armed Services, November 2, 2011," available at http://armedservices.house.gov/index.cfm/files/serve? File_id=faad05df-9016-42c5-86bc-b83144c635c9.

139 "New RF-US agreement to replace START to be concluded before year end – FM," ITAR-TASS, March 9, 2009, available at http://www.itar-tass.com/eng/level2.html?NewsID=14295189& PageNum=1.

139 Aleksey Arbatov, "Tactical Nuclear Weapons: Problems and Solutions: Strategic Offensive Weapon Reductions Could Extend to Nonstrategic Munitions," Voyenno-Promyshlenny Nezavisimoye Online, May 20, 2011, available at http://www.dialog.com/proquestdialog/.: Aleksey Arbatov, "'Concepts': Nonstrategic Nuclear Weapons; Dilemmas and Approaches; The Path to a Nuclear-Free World Promises To Be Long," Moscow Nezavisimoye Voyennoye Obozreniye Online, May 20, 2011. (Translated by World News Connection).; "In a Broad Context," Krasnaya Zvezda Online, April 29, 2011. (Translated by World News Connection).

16-17.: Payne and Foster et. al., Russian Strategy Expansion, Crisis and Conflict, op. cit., p. 91.

140 "Daily Press Briefings: Daily Press Briefing - July 29, 2014," available at http://www.state.gov/r/pa/prs/dpb/2014 /07/229907.htm.

141 Adherence to and Compliance With Arms Control, on Proliferation, and Disarmament Agreements and Commitments, (Washington D.C.: U.S. Department of State, July 2014), p. 8, available at http: //www.state.gov/documents/organization/230108.pdf.

142 Mark B. Schneider, "Russian Violations of Its Arms Control Obligations," Comparative Strategy, September 22, 2012, pp. 337-338, available at http://www.tandfonline.com/doi/abs/10.1080/01495933.2012.711115?prevSearch =%255BAbs ract%253A%2Brussia*%2Bmilitary%255D&searchHistoryKey=.

143 "Академик Евгений Николаевич Аврорин: «Наука — это то, что можно сделать, а техническая наука — это то, что нужно сделать»," atomic-energy.ru, April 10, 2013, available at http://www.atomic-energy.ru/interviews/ 2013/04/10/41068. (In Russian).

144 Alexander Vershbow, "NATO and Russia: Why Transparency is Essential," NATO, August 16, 2016, available at http://www.nato.int/cps/en/natohq/opinions_134436.htm.

145 "Secretary of Defense Dick Cheney, General Colin Powell, Chairman JCS, Pete Wilson, ASD (Public Affairs) Saturday28, 1991—10:00am," mimeo, pp. 2-3.

146 Sydney J. Freedberg Jr., "Russians 'Closed The Gap' For A2/AD: Air Force Gen. Gorenc," Breaking Defense, September 14, 2015, available at http://breakingdefense.com/2015/09/russians-closed-the-gap-for-a2ad-air-force-gen-gorenc/.

147 "Rep. Mike D. Rogers Holds a Hearing on Nuclear Deterrent Modernization Plans and Budgets," Political Transcript Wire, July 16, 2016, available at http://dialog.proquest.com/professional/login.

148 Philip Goodall, My Target Was Leningrad (UK: Fonthill Media Limited, 2015), p. 159.

149 Mark B. Schneider and Peter Huessy, "Russian Deployment of Missile Defenses Hidden in Plain Sight," Gatestone Institute, February 18, 2013, available at http://www.gatestoneinstitute.org/3590/russia-missile-defense.

150 Bill Gertz, "Inside the Ring - Russian missile defense," The Washington Times, January 5, 2011, available at http: //www.washingtontimes.com/news/2011/jan/5/inside-the-ring-442522451/?page=all.

151 "Russia to test new A-235 missile defence system in 2013 – paper," Interfax, December 19, 2012, available at http://dialog.proquest.com/professional/index.

152 "Russia: Interview With Chief of Russian Federation Air Force Air Defense Maj-Gen Viktor Gumennyy Russia: Interview With Chief of Russian Federation Air Force Air Defense Major-General Viktor Vasilyevich Gumennyy by Aleksandr Pinchuk," Krasnaya Zvezda Online, April 26, 2013. (Translated by World News Connection).: Schneider and Huessy, "Russian Deployment of Missile Defenses Hidden in Plain Sight," op. cit.: "Army; S-500 missile system will be completed on time, surpass foreign analogs – ministry," Interfax, September 5, 2012, available at http:// dialog.proquest.com/professional/login.; "Russia: Surface-to-Air Missile Troops Commander Sergey Popov Speaks: Interview with Major-General Sergey Popov, Air Force Deputy Chief Commander for the Air Defense, by Anatoliy Yermolin on Ekho Moskvy Radio Military Council program 10 Sep, 2011," available at http ://dialog.proquest.com/ professional/login.; "Russia: CINC Air Force Taken to Task for 'Wild Optimism' About PAK FA, S-500 Article by Sergey Mikhaylov especially for Stoletiye: Phantoms in Russia's Sky: We Want To Defend With SAM Systems Without Missiles and To Fly in Fighters Without 'Their Own' Engine," Stoletiye.ru Monday, July 26, 2010, available at http://dialog.proquest.com/professional/login.; "S-500 to be Russia's response to U.S. missile defense network - Defense Ministry," Interfax-AVN, November 29, 2013. (Transcribed by World News Connection).; "S-500 to be Russia's response to U.S. missile defense network - Defense Ministry," Interfax-AVN, November 29, 2013. (Transcribed by World News Connection).

153 "Deputy Defense Minister: Russia's new S-500 system to destroy any target at any altitude," TASS, March 26, 2015, available at http://en.itar-tass.com/russia/725453.

154 "Russia: Comments by Deputy Defense Minister Ostapenko on Aerospace Defense Troops Programs Commentary by Interfaks-AVN, Moscow, 24 April: The New S-500 Air Defense Missile System Will Be Able To Effectively Combat Advanced Offensive Aerospace Weapons a(euro)," Interfax-AVN Online, April 26, 2013. (Translation by World News Connection).

155 Vasiliy Sychev, "Race of shields," Lenta.ru, July 21, 2010. (Translated by World News Connection).

156 "Army; Delivery of brand new S-500 systems to Russian Aerospace Forces to begin shortly - deputy commander," Interfax, April 15, 2016, available at http://dialog.proquest.com/professional/login.

157 Ilya Kramnik, "Russia waiting for S-500 air defense system," ruvr.ru, April 9, 2012, available at http://english. Ruvr.ru/2012_04_09/71180406/.

158 Ibid.

159 Maxim Pyadushkin, "Russian Long-Range Air Defense Efforts Bloom," Aviationweek.com, March 9, 2011, available at http://www.aviationweek.com/aw/generic/story.jsp?id=news/awst/2011/03/07/AW_03_0 7_ 2011_p32-293478.xml&headline=Russian%20Long-Range%20Air%20Defense%20Efforts%20Bloom&channel =defense.: "Russia to have 10 S-500, 56 S-400 air defence battalions – official," BBC Monitoring Former Soviet Union, February 11, 2011, available at http://dialog.proquest.com/professional/login.; "Invincible Shield: Russia Puts S-400 Systems on Combat Duty Near Moscow," Sputnik News, January 29, 2016, available at http:// sputniknews.com/military/20160129/1033904865/s-400-triumf-moscow.html.

160 "Russian army puts into service long-range missile for S-300V4 system — source," TASS, March 5, 2015, available at http://tass.ru/en/russia/781138.

161 "Range of Russian S-400V4 system with new missile reaches 400 km," TASS, May 19, 2016, available at http:// tass.ru/en/defense/876665.http://tass.ru/en/defense/876665.

162 "Works continue as planned to build S-350 air defense missile system, to be completed in due time - Russian Defense Ministry," Interfax, June 27, 2013, available at http://dialog.proquest.com/professional/login.: "Almaz-Antey Unveils S-350E Vityaz Air

Defense System," Defense-update.com, August 27, 2013, available at http:// defense-update.com/20130827_vityaz.

163 Tim Ripley, London and Jeremy Binnie, "Russia deploys S-300 to Syria," IHS Jane's Defence Weekly, October 6, 2016.   http://www.janes.com/article/64377/russia-deploys-s-300-to-syria

164 Lucas Tomlinson, "Russia deploys advanced anti-missile system to Syria for first time, US officials say," Fox News.com, October 4, 2016. http://www.foxnews.com/world/2016/10/04/russia-deploys-advanced-anti-missile-system-to-syria-for-first-time-us-officials-say.html,

165 "Russia to Create Sea-Based Missile Defense System?," Naval Today.Com, September 25, 2011, available at http://navaltoday.com/2011/09/25/russia-to-create-sea-based-missile-defense-system/Russia to Create Sea-Based Missile Defense System?.: "Media: New Destroyers to Carry S-500 Missile Defense System," Rusnavy.com, June 27, 2012, available at http://rusnavy.com/news/navy/index.php?ELEMENT_ID=15445.

166 Valery Melnikov, "Future of Russian missile defense to be based in air," Ria Novosti, August 15, 2011, available at http://en.rian.ru/mlitary_news/20110815/165792644.html.

167 "Delivery of New Sukhoi T-50 Jets to Russian Aerospace Forces to Begin 2018," Sputnik News, July 4, 2016, available at http://sputniknews.com/russia/20160704/1042396354/russia-sukhoi-t-50-deliveries.html.

168 Dr. Mark B. Schneider, "The F-35 vs. the Russian Su-35 and the PAK FA," Real Clear Defense, November 5, 2015, available at http://www.realcleardefense.com/articles/2015/11/05/the_f-35_vs_the_russian_su-35_and_the_ pak_fa_108649.html.

169 "Geopolitics': Missile Defense Has Become a Religion for the United States: What Keeps Moscow and Washington From Coming to an Agreement," Nezavisimoye Voyennoye Obozreniye Online Saturday, September 22, 2012. (Translated by World News Connection).

170 Alexander Mladenov, "Access Denied Fortifying Putin's Skies," Air Forces Monthly, Issue 334, January 2016, pp. 68-69.

171 "Putin Signs a National Security Strategy of Defiance and Pushback," Eurasia Daily Monitor, Vol.13 Issue 4, January 7, 2016 available at

http://www.jamestown.org/single/?tx_ttnews%5Btt_news%5D=44953&no_cache
=1#.V7HuYaJOyUk.

172 Bill Gertz, "U.S. intelligence detects dozens of hardened bunkers for leaders," The
Washington Free Beacon, August 15, 2016, available at http://freebeacon.com/national-
security/russia-building-new-underground-nuclear-command-posts/.

173 Schneider, "Nuclear Deterrence in the Context of the European Security Crisis and
Beyond," op. cit., p. 6.

174 Colin S. Gray, "SALT I Aftermath: Have the Soviets Been Cheating?" Air Force
Magazine, December 1975, p. 29.

175 William Schneider, "Arms Control: The Lesson of Russia's Serial Treaty Violations," The
Hudson Institute, September 16, 2014, available at
http://www.hudson.org/research/10613-arms-control-the-lesson-of-russia-s-serial-treaty-
violations.

176 Soviet Noncompliance with Arms Control Agreements, Special Report 136 (Washington,
D.C.: U.S. Department of State, December 1985), p. 2.

177 Ibid.

178 "H.R. 1735—FY16 National Defense Authorization Bill Subcommittee On Strategic
Forces," April 24, 2014, available at
http://docs.house.gov/Committee/Calendar/ByEvent.aspx?EventID=103288.

179 "Statement of Robert Scher Assistant Secretary of Defense For Strategy, Plans, and
Capabilities Before the House Armed Services Subcommittee on Strategic Forces March
2, 2016," op. cit., p. 3.

180 "Russia today is not interested in U.S.-proposed arms reduction - Sergei Ivanov," Interfax,
March 5, 2013. (Transcribed by World News Connection).

181 For details on New START see "An Independent Assessment of New START Treaty,"
Heritage Foundation, April 30, 2010, available at http://www.heritage.org/
Research/Reports/2010/04/An.hes-european-defense-system_593839.: Mark B.
Schneider, "New START: The Anatomy of a Failed Negotiation," (Fairfax Va.: National
Institute Press, 2012), chapters 1-2, available at http://www.nipp.org/wp-
content/uploads/2014/12/New-start.pdf.

182 Pavel Felgenhauer, "Russia Seeks to Impose New ABM Treaty on the US by Developing BMD," Eurasia Daily Monitor Volume: 7 Issue: 136 July 16, 2010, available at http://www.jamestown. org/single/?no_cache=1&tx_ttnews[tt_news]=36624.

183 Mark B. Schneider, Confirmation of Russian Violation and Circumvention of the INF Treaty, National Institute Information Series, No. 360, (Fairfax, VA: National Institute for Public Policy, February 2014), p. 18, available at http://www.nipp.org/wp-content/uploads/2014/11/Confirmation-of-Russian-Violations-of-the-INF-Treaty8.pdf.

184 Ibid., pp. 5-6.

185 Mark B. Schneider & Keith B. Payne, "Russia Appears to Be Violating the INF Treaty," National Review.com, July 28, 2014, available at http://www.nationalreview.com/article/383839/russia.

186 "Doomsday Weapon: Russia's New Missile Shocks and Dazzles US, China," Sputnik News, March 9, 2016, available at http://sputniknews.com/russia/20160309/1036002714/russia-missile-shocker.html.

187 Schneider and Payne, "Russia Appears to Be Violating the INF Treaty," op. cit.

188 Jacek Durkalec, "Russia's Violation of the INF Treaty: Consequences for NATO," No. 107 (702), The Polish Institute for International Affairs, August 13, 2014, pp. 1-2, available at https://www.pism.pl/files/?id_plik=17932.

189 "Баллистическая ракета РС-26 'Рубеж' будет принята на вооружение Ракетных войск стратегического назначения в 2017 году, сообщил РИА Новости источник в российском военном ведомстве," Rgu.ru, March 11, 2016, available at http://rg.ru/2016/05/11/raketu-rubezh-postaviat-na-dezhurstvo-cherez-god.html. (In Russian).

190 "Press Roundtable at Interfax—Stephen G. Rademaker, Assistant Secretary of State for Arms Control, Moscow, Russia, October 6, 2004," available at http://2001-2009.state.gov/t/isn/rls/rm/37275.htm.: Schneider, "Russian Violations of Its Arms Control Obligations," op. cit., pp. 337-338.

191 Ibid.

192 Schneider, "Russian Violations of Its Arms Control Obligations," op. cit., p. 336.

193 Goodal, "My Target Was Liningrad," op. cit., p. 159.

194 "Fact Sheet U.S. Missile Defense Policy A "Phased, Adaptive Approach for Missile Defense in Europe," The White House, September 17, 2009, available at

https://www.whitehouse.gov/the-press-office/fact-sheet-us-missile-defense-policy-a-phased-adaptive-approach-missile-defense-eur.

195 Michaela Dodge, "New Strategic Arms Reduction Treaty: Time to Stop the Damage to U.S. National Security," Backgrounder, No. 3078 (Heritage Foundation June 20, 2016), available at http://www.heritage.org/research/ reports/2016/06/new-strategic-arms-reduction-treaty-time-to-stop-the-damage-to-us-national-security.

196 "START-3 Gives Russia Prestige and Levers of Influence," Izvestiya Online (Moscow Edition), January 26, 2011. (Translation by World News Connection).

197 Payne and Foster, et. al., Russian Strategy: Expansion, Crisis and Conflict, op. cit., pp. 33.

198 Robert Bridge, "Border Alert: Nuke war risk rising, Russia warns," RT, November 17, 2011, available at http://rt. com/politics/makarov-nuclear-russia-nato-575/.

199 "Treaty With Russia On Measures For Further Reduction And Limitation Of Strategic Offensive Arms (The New Start Treaty)," Senate Foreign Relations Committee, October 2010, p. 112, available at http:// foreign.senate.gov/treaties/details/?id=1668ace8-5056-a032-526a-29c8fc32e1dc.

200 "Putin orders suspension of plutonium utilization deal with US — decree," TASS, October 3, 2016, available at http://tass.com/politics/903673.

201 Andrew Kramer, "Vladimir Putin Exits Nuclear Security Pact, Citing 'Hostile Actions' by U.S," The New York Times, October 4, 2016, available at http://dialog.proquest.com/professional/login.

202 Andrew Monaghan, "The 'War' in Russia's 'Hybrid Warfare,'" Parameters, Volume 45, Number 4, Winter 2015-16, p. 72.

203 Keir Giles, Russia's New Tools for Confronting the West: Continuity and Innvation in Mscow's Exercise of Power, Research Paper, Chatham House, March 2016; Tomasz Smura and Rafał Lipka The Modernization Program of the Armed Forces of the Russian Federation –Current Status and Prospects of Success, Casimir Pulaski Foundation, January 1, 2015; Keir Giles and Dr. Andrew Monaghan, Russian Military Transformation - Goal In Sight? Strategic Studies Intitute, May 2014;

204 Michael R. Gordon, "NATO Commander Says He Sees Potent Threat from Russia," New York Times, April 2, 2014

205 Stephen Blank, "A Military Assessment of the Russian War in Ukraine," Testimony Presented to the Senate Foreign Relations Committee, Subcommittee on Europe and

Regional Security Cooperation, March 4, 2015. Also, Stephen Blank, "Russia's Hybrid War: Through a Glass Darkly," Kiev Post, April 14, 2016

206 Andrew Osorn, "Russia to build permanent Syrian naval base, eyes other outposts," Reuters, October 10, 2016. http://www.reuters.com/article/us-mideast-crisis-syria-russia-tartus-idUSKCN12A0W6?il=0

207 Cam Kasopoglu, Russia's Renewed Military Thinking: Non-Linear Warfare and Reflexive Control, Research Paper, NATO Defense College, No. 121, November 2015

208 Phillip Karber and Joshua Thibeault, Russia's New Generation Warfare, Potomac Foundation, May 13, 2016.

209 Smuza and Linka, op cit. Also Dmitry Gorenburg, Russia's State Armaments Program 2020: Is the Third Time the Charm for Military Modernization? PONARS Eurasia Policy Memo No. 125; Maria Martens, Russian Military Modernization, Science and Technology Committee, NATO Parliamentary Committee, October 11, 2015

210 David Johnson, "The Russian Invasion of Ukraine," in Headquarters, Department of the Army, The U.S. Army Combat Vehicle Modernization Strategy, January 5, 2016, p. 15.

211 Colonel (ret.) James B. Hickey, Senior Military Advisor, Senate Armed Services Committee, "Statement for the Ground Vehicle Systems Engineering and Technology Symposium," August 2, 2016

212 Karber and Thibeault, op. cit.

213 "Interview: Lt. Gen. Ben Hodges," Defense News.com, March 27, 2015. http://www.defensenews.com/story/defense/policy-budget/leaders/interviews/2015/03/27/lt-gen-ben-hodges/70573420/

214 Sidney Freedberg, Jr., "Russian Drone Threat: Army Seeks Ukraine Lesson," Breaking Defense, October 14, 2015

215 Bret Perry, "How NATO Can Disrupt Russia's New Way of War," DefenseOne, March 3, 2016.

216 Sam Gardner, The Re-Invasion of the Baltic States: Russia's Military Threat, Strategy and Capabilities, Briefing, May 9, 2016.

217 Stephen J. Blank, "A Clinic on Clausewitz," op. cit., p. 35.

218 Rick Gladstone, "Air Force General Says Russia Missile Defense Very Serious," The New York Times, January 11, 2016; Douglas Barrie, "Russia and Anti-Access/Area Denial Capabilities," Military Balance Blog, February 8, 2016.

219 Dave Majumdar, "Can America Crush Russia's A2/AD Bubbles," The National Interest, June 29, 2016.

220 "Russia ramping up military drills to Cold War levels, NATO says," Fox News, February 5, 2016.

221 Stephen J. Blank, "What Do the Zapad 2013 Exercises Reveal? (Part One)," Eurasia Daily Monitor, Volume 10, Number 177, October 2014.

222 Stephen J. Blank, "Imperial Ambitions: Russia's Military Buildup," World Affairs, May/June 2015

223 Jamie Seidel, "Russian media boasts of its new Satan II ICBM missiles' devastating power," News Corp Australia Network, May, 11, 2016.
http://www.news.com.au/technology/russian-media-boasts-of-its-new-satan-ii-icbm-missiles-devastating-power/news-story/dcfb48956097210846fc064fbbecf86f

224 Amy F. Woolf, Russian Compliance with the Intermediate Range Nuclear Forces (INF) Treaty: Background and Issues for Congress, Congressional Research Service April 13, 2016, p. 1

225 Woolf, op. cit., p. 18

226 Stephen J. Blank, "What Do the Zapad 2013 Exercises Reveal? (Part One)," op.cit. , p. 33.

227 "Russia moves nuclear-capable missiles into Kaliningrad," Reuters, October 6, 2016.
http://www.reuters.com/article/us-russia-usa-missiles-confirm-idUSKCN1280IV

228 House of Commons Defence Committee, "Towards the next Defence and Security Review: Part Two – NATO," Third Report of Session 2014-15, July 31, 2014, p. 17,
http://www.publications.parliament.uk/pa/cm201415/cmselect/cmdfence/358/358.pdf.

229 Keir Giles, Russia's 'New' Tools for Confronting the West Continuity and Innovation in Moscow's Exercise of Power, Research Paper, Russia and Eurasia Programme, Chatham House, March 2016, p. 19.

230 Lee Edwards and Elizabeth Edwards Spalding, "How Ronald Reagan Won the Cold War," Breitbart.com, February 29, 2016. http://www.breitbart.com/big-government/2016/02/29/how-ronald-reagan-won-the-cold-war/

231 Andrew Osborn, "And If Things Weren't Bad Enough, Professor Predicts End of U.S.," Wall Street Journal, December 29, 2008.
http://online.wsj.com/article/SB123051100709638419.html

232 ibid

233 " March 2012: Media warfare targets Putin's legitimacy," RT, March 10, 2012. http://rt.com/politics/putin-rally-west-panarin-237/

234 Unrestricted Warfare, by Qiao Liang and Wang Xiangsui (Beijing: PLA Literature and Arts Publishing House, February 1999). Citation is from CIA translation, pages 51-52, available at http://www.cryptome.org/cuw.htm.

235 Ibid, page 224

236 Scott Rose and Olga Tanas, "Putin Turns Black Gold to Bullion as Russia Outbuys World," Bloomberg.com, February 11, 2013. http://www.bloomberg.com/news/2013-02-10/putin-turns-black-gold-into-bullion-as-russia-out-buys-world.html?utm_source=GraphicMail

237 "Russia tried to force a bailout of Fannie and Freddie, Paulson writes," Bloomberg News via The Denver Post, January 29, 2010. http://www.denverpost.com/2010/01/29/russia-tried-to-force-a-bailout-of-fannie-and-freddie-paulson-writes/

238 "China ready to go to war to safeguard national interests," Times of India, February 12, 2011. http://timesofindia.indiatimes.com/world/china/China-ready-to-go-to-war-to-safeguard-national-interests/articleshow/7482264.cms

239 http://www.thezimbabwemail.com/zimbabwe/7824.html

240 http://www.rediff.com/news/1998/dec/21rus.htm

241 http://english.pravda.ru/russia/politics/05-06-2012/121315-putin_china-0/#

242 Fred Weir, "With US-Russia relationship toxic, Moscow looks to strengthen ties with China," Christian Science Monitor, March 22, 2013. http://www.csmonitor.com/World/Europe/2013/0322/With-US-Russia-relationship-toxic-Moscow-looks-to-strengthen-ties-with-China?nav=87-frontpage-entryNineItem

243 Gwynn Guilford, "Russia's government has become the world's largest buyer of gold, driven by fears of currency cataclysm," QZ.com, February 11, 2013. http://qz.com/52623/russias-government-has-become-the-worlds-largest-buyer-of-gold-driven-by-fears-of-currency-cataclysm/

244 Osborn, op.sit.

245 Liu Chang, "Commentary: U.S. fiscal failure warrants a de-Americanized world," Xinhua News English, October 13, 2013. http://news.xinhuanet.com/english/indepth/2013-10/13/c_132794246.htm

246 "Russia's secret weapon: crashing US economy by collapsing petrodollar," Voice of Russia Radio, March 28, 2014.

https://sputniknews.com/voiceofrussia/news/2014_03_28/Russia-s-secret-weapon-crashing-US-economy-by-collapsing-petrodollar-5071/

247 "Russia prepares to attack the petrodollar," Voice of Russia, April 4, 2014.

https://sputniknews.com/voiceofrussia/2014_04_04/Russia-prepares-to-attack-the-petrodollar-2335/

248 Bruno Waterfield, "Cyprus agrees €10bn bail-out deal with Eurozone," London Telegraph, March 25, 2013. http://www.telegraph.co.uk/finance/financialcrisis/9951680/Cyprus-agrees-10bn-bail-out-deal-with-eurozone.html

249 "Rich Russians Hurt By Cyprus Bank Bailout," NPR.org, March 26, 2013.

http://www.npr.org/2013/03/26/175335266/rich-russians-hurt-by-cyprus-bank-bailout

250 Richard Becker, "IMF/World Bank, Globalization and US Militarism," International Action Center, March 26, 2000. http://www.iacenter.org/folder02/imfworld.htm

251 "BRICS plan new $50bn bank to rival World Bank and IMF," RT.com, March 26, 2013.

http://rt.com/business/bank-rival-imf-world-852/

252 Ryan Villarreal, "So Long, Yankees! China and Brazil Ditch US Dollar in Trade Deal Before BRICS Summit," International Business Times, March 26, 2013.

http://www.ibtimes.com/so-long-yankees-china-brazil-ditch-us-dollar-trade-deal-brics-summit-1153415

253 ibid

254 ibid

255 Jonathan Weisman, "At Global Economic Gathering, U.S. Primacy Is Seen as Ebbing," New York Times, April 17, 2015.

http://www.nytimes.com/2015/04/18/business/international/at-global-economic-gathering-concerns-that-us-is-ceding-its-leadership-role.html?_r=0

256 Lawrence Summers, "The US may have lost its role as the world's economic leader," Washington Post, April 6, 2015.

257 Tyler Durden, "China Completes SWIFT Alternative, May Launch 'De-Dollarization Axis' As Soon As September," ZeroHedge.com, March 9, 2015.

http://www.zerohedge.com/news/2015-03-09/

258 Nicholas Borst, "CIPS and the International Role of the Renminbi," Pacific Exchange Blog, January 27, 2016. http://www.frbsf.org/banking/asia-program/pacific-exchange-blog/cips-and-the-international-role-of-the-renminbi/

259 "US warns of hacking threat to interbank payment network," BBC.com, June 7, 2016. http://www.bbc.com/news/business-36473912

260 "Ruble-yuan settlements booming, set to reshape global finance," RT.com, June 16, 2015. https://www.rt.com/business/254305-russia-china-trade-business/

261 "Foreign Central Banks Allowed to Open Yuan Settlement Accounts in China," Hong Kong Trade Development Council, November 19, 2015. http://hkmb.hktdc.com/en/1X0A4A33/hktdc-research/Foreign-Central-Banks-Allowed-to-Open-Yuan-Settlement-Accounts-in-China

262 Tyler Turden, "DoD Admits US Global Hegemony Threatened By China, Russia In "Persistently Disordered World," ZeroHendge.com, June 30, 2016. http://www.zerohedge.com/news/2016-07-30/dod-admits-us-global-hegemony-threatened-china-russia-persistently-disordered-world

263 "US breakup: Myth or reality?" RT.com, October 27, 2011. https://www.rt.com/politics/panarin-usa-collapse-economy-905/

264 Kevin Begos, "Next cold war? Gas drilling boom rattles Russia," Associate Press via the Deseret News, September 30, 2012. http://www.deseretnews.com/article/765608155/Next-cold-war-Gas-drilling-boom-rattles-Russia.html

265 "Exclusive Interview with Former KGB Agent -- Part 2," LasVegasNow.com, July 6, 2001. http://www.lasvegasnow.com/news/exclusive-interview-with-former-kgb-agent-part-2

266 "Meet the lizard that will kill Texas oil production," Hot Air.com, June 1, 2011. http://hotair.com/archives/2011/06/01/meet-the-lizard-that-will-kill-texas-oil-production/

267 Jim Forsyth, "Conservation deal keeps sand dune lizard off U.S. endangered list," Reuters, June 13, 2012. http://www.reuters.com/article/2012/06/13/us-usa-environment-lizard-idUSBRE85C1M720120613

268 Selam Gebrekidan, "Permian Basin oil output to jump 60 pct by 2016-Bentek," Reuters, August 15, 2012. http://www.reuters.com/article/2012/08/15/permian-oil-bentek-idUSL2E8JFCS120120815

269 Lachlan Markay, "Matt Damon's Anti-Fracking Movie Financed by Oil-Rich Arab Nation," Daily Signal, September 28, 2012. http://blog.heritage.org/2012/09/28/matt-damons-anti-fracking-movie-financed-by-oil-rich-arab-nation/

270 Kirit Radia, "Polish President's Plane Crash Was Assassination, His Brother Says," abcnews.com, March 29, 2012. http://abcnews.go.com/blogs/headlines/2012/03/polish-presidents-plane-crash-was-assassination-his-brother-says/

271 Matt Clinch, "How the US Shale Gas Boom Could Derail China," CNBC.com, March 7, 2013. http://www.cnbc.com/id/100531212

272 Robert Kahn, "The Russian Crisis: Early Days," Global Economics Monthly, Council on Foreign Relations, January 2015.
http://www.cfr.org/about/newsletters/archive/newsletter/n2493

273 "Saudi Arabia Offers Russia Economic Incentives to Drop Assad," Moscow Times, June 22, 2016. https://themoscowtimes.com/news/saudi-arabia-to-make-russia-more-powerful-than-ussr-to-end-assad-support-54705

274 Wang Wei, "How Russian Hackers Placed "Digital Bomb" Into the NASDAQ," Hacker News, July 20, 2014. http://thehackernews.com/2014/07/how-russian-hackers-placed-digital-bomb.html

275 "Michael Lewis 'retries' former Goldman Sachs programmer Sergey Aleynikov," MarketWatch.com, August 1, 2013.
http://blogs.marketwatch.com/thetell/2013/08/01/michael-lewis-retries-former-goldman-sachs-programmer-sergey-aleynikov/

276 Deborah Jacobs, "Why We Could Easily Have Another Flash Crash," Forbes.com, August 9, 2013. http://www.forbes.com/sites/deborahljacobs/2013/08/09/why-we-could-easily-have-another-flash-crash/#630a25205fe4

277 Jim McTague, "How Foreigners Could Disrupt U.S. Markets," Barron's, September 11, 2010.

278 Robert Lenzner, "Some Foreign Nations Have The Cyberwar Capability To Destroy Our Financial System, NSA Admits," Forbes.com, December 15, 2013.
http://www.forbes.com/sites/robertlenzner/2013/12/15/some-foreign-nations-have-cyberwar-capability-to-destroy-our-financial-system-nsa-admits/#6c19afff5b81

279 Kevin Freeman, "What More Proof Do We Need? Preparing an American Response," Global Economic Warfare.com, January 27, 2015.

http://globaleconomicwarfare.com/2015/01/what-more-proof-do-we-need-preparing-an-american-response/

280 Owen Matthews, "Russia's Greatest Weapon May Be Its Hackers," Newsweek, May 7, 2015. http://www.newsweek.com/2015/05/15/russias-greatest-weapon-may-be-its-hackers-328864.html

281 Joe Uchill, "Administration vows 'proportional' response to Russian hack," The Hill, October 11, 2016. http://thehill.com/policy/cybersecurity/300451-administration-response-to-russia-will-be-proportional-not-announced-in

282 Lenoid Bershidsky, "Russians Have Learned How to Hack Power Grids," Bloomberg.com, January 7, 2016. https://www.bloomberg.com/view/articles/2016-01-07/russians-have-learned-how-to-hack-power-grids

283 Ted Koppel, Lights Out: A Cyberattack, A Nation Unprepared, Surviving the Aftermath. (New York, Crown, 2015), p. 8.

284 R. James Woolsey and Peter Vincent Pry, "The Growing Threat From an EMP Attack," Wall Street Journal, August 12, 2014.

285 Ibid.

286 Dmitry Kiselev, "Russia and the West are trading places on freedom of speech," London Guardian, April 10, 2014.

287 Peter Pomerantsev and Michael Weiss, "The Menace of Unreality: How the Kremlin Weaponizes Information, Culture and Money" Institute of Modern Russia, 2015. http://www.interpretermag.com/wp-content/uploads/2015/07/PW-31.pdf

288 Ibid.

289 "Russia sets up offshore drilling rigs in Ukraine Black Sea waters," Ukraine Today, July 25, 2016. http://uatoday.tv/politics/russia-sets-up-offshore-drilling-rigs-on-ukraine-s-gas-oil-fields-video-703616.html

290 "Black Sea offshore production in 2015 – a route to energy independence?" ITE Oil and Gas, April 1, 2015. http://www.oilgas-events.com/market-insights/georgia-romania-russia-turkey/black-sea-offshore-production-in-2015-a-route-to-energy-independence-/801781383

291 William Broad, "In Taking Crimea, Putin Gains a Sea of Fuel Reserves," New York Times, May 17, 2014. http://www.nytimes.com/2014/05/18/world/europe/in-taking-crimea-putin-gains-a-sea-of-fuel-reserves.html?_r=0

292 Carol Matlack, "Losing Crimea Could Sink Ukraine's Offshore Oil and Gas Hopes," Bloomberg Business Week, March 11, 2014. http://www.bloomberg.com/news/articles/2014-03-11/losing-crimea-could-sink-ukraines-offshore-oil-and-gas-hopes

293 Jim Langers, "Exxon Mobil puts Ukraine gas prospect on hold." Dallas Morning News, March March 5, 2014. http://www.dallasnews.com/business/energy/20140305-exxon-mobil-puts-ukraine-gas-prospect-on-hold.ece

294 Joe Parson, "Kiev's Energy Security Threatened by Moscow," Moscow Times, March 20, 2014. https://themoscowtimes.com/articles/kievs-energy-security-threatened-by-moscow-33145

295 William Broad, op. cit.

296 Maksym Bugriy, Russia's Moves to Gain Dominance in the Black Sea, Eurasia Daily Monitor Volume: 13 Issue: 32. Jamestown Foundation, February 17, 2016.

297 Alex Leonor, "Russian hijack of Ukrainian drilling rigs could open hybrid naval blockade," Euromaidan Press, December 18, 2015. http://euromaidanpress.com/2015/12/18/a-hybrid-naval-blockade/#arvlbdata

298 http://static.kremlin.ru/media/events/files/ru/uAFi5nvux2twaqjftS5yr IZUVTJan77L.pdf

299 Eugenia Gusilov, "Ukraine's reality: upstream access denial," Romania Energy Center, December 17, 2015. http://www.roec.biz/bsad/portfolio-item/ukraines-reality-upstream-access-denial/

300 Masha Green, "Did the Soviet Union Really End?" New York Times, August 17, 2016.

301 [author name redacted], "James J. Angleton, Anatoliy Golitsyn, and the 'Monster Plot': Their Impact on CIA Personnel and Operations," Studies in Intelligence, Vol. 55, No.4, December 2011, declassified CIA article available at the National Security Archive at http://nsarchive.gwu.edu/NSAEBB/NSAEBB493/docs/intell_ebb_025.PDF.

302 Greg Miller, "As Russia reasserts itself, U.S. intelligence agencies focus anew on the Kremlin," Washington Post, September 14, 2016.

303 Mikhail Gorbachev, October and Perestroika: the Revolution Continues. (Moscow: Novosti Press Agency Publishing. House, 1987)

304 Robert Buchar, And Reality Be Damned... Undoing America: What Media Didn't Tell You about the End of the Cold War and the Fall of Communism in Europe. (Strategic Book Publishing & Rights Agency, 2010).

305 "Exclusive: Key General Splits With Obama Over Ukraine," The Daily Beast, April 11, 2014. http://www.thedailybeast.com/articles/2014/04/11/exclusive-key-general-splits-with-obama-over-ukraine.html.

306 "Hacked Former NATO General Defends Plotting to Push Obama to Escalate Tensions With Russia," The Intercept, July 6, 2016. https://theintercept.com/2016/07/06/hacked-former-nato-general-defends-plotting-to-push-obama-to-escalate-tensions-with-russia/

307 Cliff Kincaid et al, Back from the Dead: The Return of the Evil Empire. (Create Space, 2014)

308 Putin sang the KGB unofficial anthem with the Russian spies who were deported from the U.S. in 2010 shortly after their arrival in Russia;

Putin has praised the work of Soviet spies (such as Julius and Ethel Rosenberg, who stole U.S. atom bomb secrets for the Russians); a plaque dedicated to Kim Philby, a Russian double agent, was placed on the wall outside Russia's foreign intelligence service headquarters

Soviet Red Star markings have returned to Russian military aircraft;

the cruiser Aurora, which played an important role in the Bolshevik Revolution of 1917, was made into a museum.

309 Damien Sharkov, "Russia's Putin: I've Always Liked Communist And Socialist 'Ideas,'" Newsweek.com, January 25, 2016. http://www.newsweek.com/russias-putin-says-he-always-liked-communist-socialist-ideas-419289

310 Bella V. Dodd, School of Darkness, page 233.

311 The book, available from Amazon.com, examines the educational background of former Secretary of State Hillary Clinton, in a chapter titled, "From Goldwater Girl to Marxist," and looks at the far-left influences at Harvard and Columbia that have guided President Barack Obama's "fundamental transformation" of the United States.

312 M. Stanton Evans, "McCarthyism by the numbers," Human Events, January 29, 2014. http://humanevents.com/2014/01/29/mccarthyism-by-the-numbers/

313 See "The Red Diaper Baby in Obama's Red Cover-Up," http://www.aim.org/special-report/the-red-diaper-baby-in-obamas-red-cover-up/

314 Benjamin B. Fischer, "Doubles Troubles: The CIA and Double Agents during the Cold War," International Journal of Intelligence and Counterintelligence, 29: 48-74, 2016.

315 For more information on the film "The Collapse of Communism: The Untold Story," go to http://www.collapseofcommunism.com/home.html

316 Claudette Roulo, "Breedlove: Russian Actions Bring Europe to Decisive Point," American Forces Press Service, June 30, 2014.

http://archive.defense.gov/news/newsarticle.aspx?id=122576

317 Lisa, Ferinando, "Breedlove: Russia, Instability Threaten U.S., European Security Interests," DoD News, February 25, 2016.

http://www.defense.gov/News/Article/Article/673338/breedlove-russia-instability-threaten-us-european-security-interests

318 Transcript available at http://edition.cnn.com/TRANSCRIPTS/1604/12/cg.02.html

319 Mark LaRochelle, "Yes, OSS Was Riddled With Communists," Human Events July 23, 2007. http://humanevents.com/2007/07/23/yes-oss-was-riddled-with-communists/

320 President Reagan visited the headquarters of the NSA in 1986 and strongly endorsed the work of the agency that is tasked with conducting surveillance of America's foreign enemies. The NSA's National Cryptologic Museum includes materials from that period, including a transcript of Reagan's remarks. There also exists a video of Reagan's dedication of new buildings at the agency complex at Fort George H. Meade, Maryland, that has been posted online by America's Survival, Inc.

321 For more information on the movie "The Enemies Within" go to http://enemieswithinmovie.com/preorder/.